Inside the Promised Land

Inside the Promised Land

A personal view of today's Israel

Gerald Kaufman

Wildwood House

First published in Great Britain in 1986
by Wildwood House Ltd
Gower House, Croft Road,
Aldershot, Hants GU11 3HR,
England

British Library Cataloguing in Publication Data

Kaufman, Gerald
    Inside the Promised Land.
    1. Israel—History
    I. Title
    956.94′054   DS126.5
    ISBN 0-7045-3074-0
        0-7045-0536-3 (paperback)

Typeset in Great Britain by
Guildford Graphics Limited, Petworth, West Sussex.
Printed in Great Britain at the University Press, Cambridge.

Contents

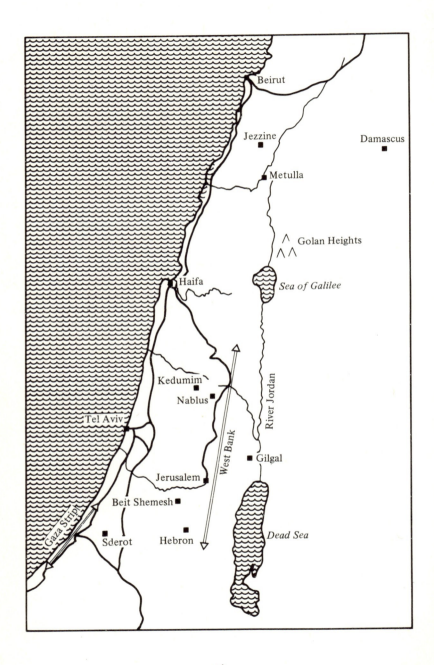

Preface

'Come with me', said my kibbutznik friend Benny, 'and I will show you a miracle.'

Since we were in the Holy Land – indeed, in Jerusalem itself – the prospect of a miracle seemed not only appropriate but perfectly natural. I therefore readily seated myself in the small car we had hired, and we drove to the Hill of Evil Counsel, at the top of which, after the Israeli War of Independence of 1948, was sited the local headquarters of the United Nations.

As the road snaked sinuously upwards towards the crest of the Hill, Benny without warning stopped the car, changed into neutral, and took his foot off the brake. Free-wheeling, the car under its own momentum instantly began running uphill. I was amazed; Benny was smug. The miracle had worked.

Of course, it was all an optical illusion. The contours of the hillside made the road appear to be going upwards when in fact it was descending. This was perfectly clear to anyone looking on from a neighbouring hill. The experience was, however, an apt symbol of what was happening to the country in which the Hill of Evil Counsel lies.

Many passengers in the Israeli car of state believe that their country is progressing upwards, steadily and optimistically. Others, with the advantage of a clearer perspective, see the land they love free-wheeling remorselessly downwards towards an abyss into which, unless the brakes can be employed speedily, all their hopes seem doomed to sink.

Introduction

The El Al Boeing 737 took off from Heathrow precisely on time. This punctuality was a disconcerting change from the days when the name of Israel's national airline was alleged to be an acronym for the slogan Every Landing Always Late. I was starting out on the latest of the trips to Israel that I had been making, regularly and frequently, for a quarter of a century. This was my thirty-fifth, possibly fortieth, journey there. I had lost count.

All the same, I was no longer sure where I was going. Of course, I knew that Israel was a tiny patch of the Levant, a corner of the Middle East, pretending that it was really a part of Western Europe or even North America. When I first went there at the beginning of the 1960s, in the thirteenth year of statehood, I was aware that the foundation of Israel in 1948 was the culmination of a long, toilsome process which had been launched with the publication at the very end of the nineteenth century of a book called *Der Judenstaat, The Jewish State*. Its author was Theodor Herzl, a Viennese journalist who, appalled at the anti-semitism surrounding the trial and degradation of the French army officer Captain Alfred Dreyfus, decided that the Jews must have a land of their own. The idea of Zionism already existed. Herzl turned it into a political objective, and it is for this reason that his remains have been transferred to a shrine on a Jerusalem hillside and his picture gazes down on the deliberations of the Knesset, the Israeli Parliament.

The baton was later picked up by Chaim Weizmann, an

Eastern European Jew who took up residence in England and lived for a time in Manchester. A house he occupied in Birchfields Road is situated in the constituency I have represented in the House of Commons since 1970, so that, in a way, I am posthumously Weizmann's Member of Parliament. During the First World War, Weizmann attracted the attention of leading politicians and wormed his way into their confidence by his scientific ingenuity. The legend is false that he was granted the Balfour Declaration as a reward for a dazzling invention which won the war. It is, however, true that at a time of deep difficulty for Britain he made a discovery that solved a shortage of acetone, a substance needed for manufacture of ammunition; and that this contribution was greatly valued by his adopted country.

It is also true that it was Weizmann who, as one of his Manchester constituents, in 1905 aroused an interest in Zionism in Arthur James Balfour, then Prime Minister, and that it was in response to Weizmann's pressure that Balfour, Foreign Secretary in the wartime coalition, in 1917 sent a letter to Lord Rothschild that became known as the Balfour Declaration. This letter included a key passage which stated: 'His Majesty's Government view with favour the establishment in Palestine of a national home for the Jewish people, and will use their best endeavours to facilitate the achievement of this object.'

No-one was ever really sure what this declaration meant precisely: whether the intention was simply to allow Jews to settle in Palestine or whether the aim was to turn Palestine, despite its overwhelmingly Arab population, into a Jewish country. The Jews, for their part, were absolutely sure what it *ought* to mean as far as they were concerned, and they tried to change the balance of population in Palestine by flooding it with Jewish immigrants. This met with resistance from many of the indigenous Arabs and, eventually, with administrative obstruction from Britain, the mandatory power which uneasily governed the country. A Conservative Government, in 1939, issued a White Paper intended to give the Arabs a veto on Jewish immigration. The Labour Government which came to office in 1945 was involved in unhappy disagreements with the Jews, who had expected much from it and were bitterly disappointed, and in 1948 washed its hands of the problem. Britain withdrew her troops and administration from Palestine, leaving its Jewish population – as many assumed – at the mercy of armies invading from the surrounding Arab countries.

Those Jews, however, had not only established an effective internal administrative system, a trade union movement, a form of communal settlement – the kibbutz village – which was the nearest the world had ever seen to communism in action, and Tel Aviv, the world's largest all-Jewish city. They had also created an underground army, Haganah, which, with difficulty and at the cost of grievous casualties, managed to defeat the Arabs. The state of Israel was declared in May 1948, by which time the 5,500 square miles offered to the Jews by an abortive United Nations partition plan in 1947 was being expanded into the 8,000 square miles which constituted the territory of the new country until it unilaterally (and with dubious legality) absorbed inside its borders East Jerusalem and the Golan Heights, both conquered in the Six Day War of 1967. Weizmann was made President of Israel, not really as a reward, more as a way of shunting him into a siding. The real authority was wielded by David Ben-Gurion, who became, and for a long time remained, the pragmatic, cynical, controversial, but indubitably dynamic Prime Minister of a troubled and troublesome nation.

Under Ben-Gurion a Law of Return was passed which allowed almost any Jew to enter Israel and, instantly, to become a citizen. Much of the remnant of European Jewry arrived, as was expected. Less expected was the mass immigration of Jews from the Arab countries of North Africa and Western Asia. Inherently economically unviable, bolstered by German reparations, assistance from the United States, and financial contributions from Jews in the diaspora, Israel thrived, however precariously, and developed into a busy little democracy. The state's military strength was also expanded, so that, in 1956, it was able (in a covert and somewhat disreputable collusion with Britain and France) to fight a victorious war with Egypt following President Nasser's nationalization of the Suez Canal.

When, not long afterwards, I paid my first visit to Israel, I lost no time in falling in love with the place. I saw it for what it was, without illusions. I was not blind to its untidiness, its inefficiency, its makeshift air. Yet I was moved by the beauty of its mountains in Galilee and its Negev desert. I was entranced by the almost supernatural ambience of Jerusalem, even though at that time I could only tour the amputated fragment of the city that lay to the west of the disgusting makeshift wall that divided it, pierced only by a transit point (through which I as a Jew could not pass) mundanely named the Mandelbaum Gate. I was impressed by the achievements in democratic administration, social progress and industrial expansion of Israel's Labour-Party-dominated coalition government. In an imperfect part of an imperfect world it was possible, quite a lot of the time, to see genuine idealism in action.

As I continued, year after year and sometimes several times a year, to travel to Israel, I made friends there. Some of these, of course, were private citizens. Others were among the country's leading personalities. The most prominent was Golda Meir, who eventually became Prime Minister, whom I met often during my visits, who generously invited me to spend a New Year holiday with her at her family kibbutz at Revivim – though, sadly, I could not go – and who on one occasion unforgettably thanked me for what she said I had done for her country. The politician I came to know best, to admire and to love, was Yigal Allon, who had been commander of the Palmach, the élitist crack military force of the kibbutzim, and who became a leading member of the cabinet, most notably as Foreign Minister. Allon should have been Prime Minister, and I often urged him, in his lovely house in Jerusalem and his even lovelier kibbutz, Ginossar, on the shores of the Sea of Galilee, to make the moves that might bring him the party leadership. He was too nice, insufficiently ruthless, to act; he died, far too young, at a time when his country sorely needed him.

At first, however, everything seemed to go from success to success. I chanced to be in Israel in May 1967, just before the Six-Day War. When Nasser closed the Straits of Tiran to Israeli shipping, anger gave way to gloom and gloom to crisis. I was there to watch the activation of the clockwork mechanism of an Israeli army mobilisation. A friend of mine, Benny, lived – and still lives – in a kibbutz at the foot of Mount Carmel. I came to know him and his wife Esterka, and their two infant sons, in the early 1960s. Benny had already fought, and been wounded, in the Suez War (Sinai War to the Israelis) of 1956. Now, together with his fellow-countrymen, he was being called to fight again. When the message came, they all just went off, quietly, almost eerily. I, feeling myself in the way, went off too, back to England.

A few days later, the Israelis attacked Egypt, and in six days decisively defeated Nasser and his Jordanian and Syrian allies. I wished I had stayed to experience those extraordinary days in Israel itself. However, even though I was back in England, I still had the opportunity to feel useful. I worked at the time in the political office of Harold Wilson, not only Prime Minister but a strong supporter of Israel. Each day during the war, and for some time afterwards, I would get into a taxi in Whitehall and go off to the Israeli Embassy at Palace Green, Kensington. There the Israeli Ambassador, Aharon Remez (who became another personal friend), would give me a comprehensive, confidential briefing on the day's events. I would then take a taxi back to Downing Street and report to Wilson, who was thus able to compare the information from the Israelis with the material supplied to him by British Intelligence (which, of course, was not made available to me).

A few days after the Israeli victory I returned to Israel to prepare a report for Wilson on the aftermath of the war. I had been asked to suggest to the Israelis that they should not make any precipitate decisions about the status of East Jerusalem, which they had just occupied. I was taken there, passing for the first time through the Mandelbaum Gate, visiting the Western Wall and David's Tower; and I was told there that the decision to annex the Eastern City had already been made. For the first time I saw Jericho and the Judean Desert. I went to the Allenby Bridge over the

Jordan and watched the forlorn and bedraggled Arab refugees waiting to cross. I talked to Levi Eshkol, the Prime Minister who had succeeded Ben-Gurion, and asked him to ensure that the refugees be treated humanely. 'Why', he demanded in exasperation, 'should such high standards be expected of Israel when they are not expected of others?' I replied: 'Because that is the way you want to be judged; you have to live up to what you expect of yourselves.'

I had a marvellous row with Yitzhak Rabin, later to be Prime Minister, then Chief of Staff of the Israel Defence Forces which had become the marvel of the world. He gave me what was supposed to be a secret briefing in his head-quarters at Hakiryah, the government compound in Tel Aviv. He told me, with justifiable pride, of the conquest of Jerusalem, of the routing of the Syrians, of the almost total destruction on the ground of the Egyptian Air Force on the first morning of the war. As he spoke, I remembered that the Israeli cover story for their pre-emptive strike against the Egyptians had been alleged detection on their radar screens of aircraft moving eastward against them. Very innocently, I asked Rabin: 'Since your action against them before they took off was so successful, whatever became of those massed Egyptian 'planes you picked up on your radar?' Rabin, very sensibly in view of his inability convincingly to answer this question, threw himself into a rage. 'Our meeting is to discuss military matters, not politics,' this contained and courteous man shouted. I did not press him further, and in later years all our meetings were amicable.

The victory in the Six-Day War made the Israelis the heroes of much of the world. It gave the nation a self-confidence it had never known before, and started off a vibrant economic boom. They did not use their victory as a starting-point for negotiating a peace. Instead, that victory bred in the Israelis an unthinking arrogance. This led them to believe that they could solve all their external problems by force of arms, and caused them to regard as subsidiary, almost marginal, the problem of how to cope with having, inside the territories they occupied, but did not annex, hundreds of thousands of Palestinian Arabs with needs but without rights. Still, I myself was infused with sufficient enthusiasm to write a book, published in 1973 to coincide with the twenty-fifth anniversary of the foundation of the state, whose title, *To Build the Promised Land,* epitomised my favourable and affirmative feelings.

Nemesis came six years later, when the Egyptians achieved the unthinkable and, in the Yom Kippur War of 1973, crossed the Suez Canal into Sinai while at the same time, in one of the most massive tank actions the world had ever seen, the Syrians invaded the Golan Heights. I had been in Israel a few days before this war, too, but no anticipation of trouble disturbed any of the politicians I met on that occasion. The Israelis won this war as well, and won it convincingly. Yet they lost their confidence, and the Labour Party, apparently the party of perpetual government, irretrievably lost support. That support was further eroded by a grievous flaw which undermined what remained of the idealism of the country's socialist movement. *Protektzia,* the use of influence for gain and advancement, had always been present in Israeli society, at once a joke and an intrusive reality. That *protektzia* too often now turned into a real corruption, involving public officials and government ministers. When an election took place in 1977, the extreme right-wing grouping Likud, led by the former terrorist Menachem Begin, gained enough seats to form a coalition that turned out Labour. In 1981 Begin won again.

As I continued my visits to Israel, I felt that I detected something increasingly disagreeable about the place. Much that I had admired, much that excited me, survived and indeed burgeoned. Yet there was a sourness, even a nastiness, which I had not previously discerned and which I thought ominous and disturbing. Partly it stemmed from the appalling economic crisis which engulfed the country. Partly it arose like a miasma from the ghastly invasion of Lebanon in 1982. Yet there was something else, something I could not define. I wanted to find out whatever I could about what was happening. I decided to go to Israel and, in the winter season of early 1985, to travel around the country, to talk to people, and simply to look and to observe.

That was why I was travelling on the Boeing 737. As its wheels rumbled down for the landing at Ben-Gurion airport, I wondered what was waiting for me.

I

The Israel Experience

The leaflet was a fetching blue, decorated brightly in red and white. THE ISRAEL EXPERIENCE, it announced, A NEW MAGICAL MULTI-MEDIA SHOW. I found it on a table outside one of the Hungarian blintz houses in Tel Aviv which are fighting a gallant rear-guard action against the encroaching hordes of American-style donut houses. I sat down, ordered an apple-and-raisin blintz obliterated by sour cream, and began to read.

'THE ISRAEL EXPERIENCE', I learned, showed 'Israel as you've never seen it before. Through computer-age technology, the Land and People of Israel are dramatically portrayed in stunning life-like color. A beautiful musical score fills the theatre from every direction, along with very special effects. Marvel at the miracle that is Israel at THE ISRAEL EXPERIENCE.' Already I could not wait, but as I read further I learned that the Israel Experience Theatre was equipped with '300 plush comfortable seats. A giant 18-meter-wide curved screen. 48 integrated pictures with over 4,000 moving slides. 3 motion picture projectors, special effects and a life-like quadrophonic sound system blended together through a centralised computer system.' Also available were tourist banking facilities, highly necessary, it seemed to me, since the price of admission for a fifty-minute show was a whopping $5. When I had first visited Israel, and for many years afterwards, prices were listed, naturally, in Israeli pounds, which eventually were transformed into shekels. Now inflation was so rampant that it was risky for shopkeepers to price in the domestic currency most goods except perishables. The U.S. dollar had spread like a plague over the land.

Still, despite the high price of admission, I was determined to see this show; and when, back at my hotel, I read in a tourist magazine that 'while tickets for screenings of The Israel Experience program can be purchased at the site, it is probably wise to be assured of them in advance', I lost no time in going along to purchase my ticket, as advised. The site was in Jaffa, which used to be a beat-up, run-down appendage of Tel Aviv but is now itself a spruced-up tourist attraction, with old Turkish slums converted into art galleries, antique shops and jewellery boutiques. Terrified that all that day's tickets for The Israel Experience would have been snapped up, I hastened in search of the Old Jaffa Mall, where The Israel Experience was located.

I came upon a dazzlingly new but very oriental-looking building which, the tourist magazine had informed me, was the outcome of an inventive architect 'melding' a new structure with an existing one 'dating from the Turkish era'. I dashed inside and there found a box-office kiosk which imprisoned a male assistant talking absorbedly on the telephone. I hopped up and down in fear that these might be the very last tickets being sold at that very moment, though even my rudimentary Hebrew indicated to me that, if the assistant was indeed in the act of making a sale, he must have very speedily got on highly affectionate terms with the prospective customer. Eventually the conversation came to an end, and the young man turned his attention to me. A ticket for the 6 p.m. performance? Yes, he thought he could manage that. He pressed the necessary buttons on his computer console, and a freshly-minted ticket edged grinning up from its aperture. I handed over my five dollars before the assistant had a chance to change his mind, and then, since it was still a little while before the start of the performance, set out to explore the rest of the building.

The leaflet had promised that the Israel Experience Theatre contained an establishment called From the Earth, a vegetarian kosher roof garden restaurant, but this did not seem to be functioning. Nor could I find an advertised object which I would dearly have liked to see, namely 'the world's biggest mezuzah'. The mezuzah is a Biblical text inscribed on parchment, which, inserted into a small case, observant Jews attach to their doorposts; the Israel Experience Theatre contained no doorpost large enough to have mounted on it the promised jumbo-sized specimen. However, a booth selling videotapes was quite busy, and I paused and inspected a showroom full of beautifully designed jewellery, none of which, curiously, was for sale. Now it was time for the performance to begin and I hurried down from the building's upper floor to the basement foyer leading to the auditorium. Not a soul was to be seen. Had I left it too late? Was the audio-visual entertainment, presented, as I now saw, by Creative Management Associates, already under way? Had I disastrously missed some of the 4,000 moving slides or the fabled special effects? I rushed, trembling, into the auditorium itself.

I discovered it to be almost as empty as the foyer. Five people were present, filling only a tiny fraction of the seats which were, as I sank down into one, as plush and comfortable as promised. Promptly, the lights dimmed. The audience, what there was of it, was complete. The audio-visual miracle was about to begin.

Music, as from the film of *Exodus*, filled the theatre, indeed enveloped it, the quadrophonic sound system being as vivid as could possibly be desired. The 65-foot-wide screen started to pulsate with colour. Out of the sea, presumably the Mediterranean, arose a vast, monstrous object. It turned out to be a voluptuous girl dressed in a bikini, both girl and exiguous garment projected at many times larger than life-size. So this was the Israel of the mid-1980s, at least as the country's publicists wished outsiders to envisage it: a land fit for the lubricious to be Peeping Toms in.

A commentator, of whom I was to have had more than my fill long before the fifty minutes were up, announced that Israel was 'small but exciting, because something is always happening here'. That, of course, was true, what with wars, demonstrations, strikes, and religious disagreements between and within all the various denominations present in this land of the Bible. Indeed, the oleaginous commentator

3

immediately went on to describe the country as 'a land of many religions all living side by side'.

We moved on. A few seconds were allotted to the Knesset, the only openly and genuinely elected Parliament between Greece and India, but here depicted as a squawling Bedlam, notable in particular for stridently vociferous women: not a monument to democracy but a joke to be tolerated indulgently. We were next shown traffic jams, street markets, fashion parades, these being accompanied by an outbreak of strobe lighting. Next there was a second or two of farming, followed by a brief section on the kibbutz movement. The kibbutzim, the collective settlements, are, of course, the suppliers of the people who are the elite in the Israeli armed forces and the country's Labour Party, as well as being a unique socialist experiment in communal living and ownership of property. They were depicted in this audio-visual presentation as places which celebrated festivals all the time and were, on the whole, also a bit of a joke.

Indeed, as The Israel Experience proceeded, what we saw was a country in which very little that was serious took place, and this was really quite appropriate, since there seemed to be no problems of any kind (apart from traffic jams). It was a land of antiquity, 'where you will be sure to find a Roman capital while ploughing', a land of tourism (with tourists treated as camera-toting idiots), a land of Christianity as well as Judaism, a land of scientific progress. There was just a hint of darker hues. A moment or two was devoted to the Holocaust in Europe under the Nazis, but no more emphasis, indeed probably less, was given to this event than to the bikini-clad giantess who had launched the film. A handful of war-planes was shown, but their necessity appeared questionable, since there was scant reference to any wars in which such equipment might have been employed, no reference whatever to any possible enemies against whom such wars might have been fought, and not the tiniest mention of a country called Lebanon.

There was no acknowledgement of the existence of the West Bank of the Jordan, let alone of settlements on the West Bank, and accordingly none that such settlements, if they existed, might be controversial; though a glimpse was provided of Orthodox Jews, depicted as picturesque additions to a landscape in which, the commentator informed the six of us in the theatre, 'we are one people'. There were hygienic pictures of industrial development, but none illustrating Israel's economic crisis. The sophisticated visual effects – which included a burst of smoke for the brief passing reference to the Yom Kippur war, a burning bush for a Biblical moment, and the whole theatre appearing to shoot up in flames for the destruction of Masada – were not employed to depict the 1,000-per cent inflation current at that moment in the Israeli state's life.

Above all, there was no mention of Arabs. Hundreds of thousands of Israeli citizens are Arabs, yet Arabs were shown (I did my best to count it) for some ten seconds without the commentator so much as explaining who or what they were. While various varieties of Judaism and Christianity were on view, there was no reference whatever to the Muslim religion; a glimpse of mosques was provided as part of the colourful Jerusalem skyline, but we were not told what these buildings were or to what use they were put.

The Israeli Experience was, in fact, a fraud. It did not begin to tell the truth about the land, but presented the state as its publicists wanted it to be seen: a colourful, picturesque, carefree, peaceful, prosperous Jewish country, making steady progress and with no problems that could not be solved by hygienically white-coated scientists, laughable politicians, or nobly altruistic rabbis. It was, indeed, depicted as a paradise on earth. Poverty, slums, strife, intolerance, enemies, wars, had all been edited out by the skills of Creative Management Associates.

The Israel Experience was over. I was back experiencing the real Israel. It was very different from what I had been watching for the previous fifty minutes, but the screen was larger than 65 feet wide and the smoke and the flames were real.

2

Right to Left

I first visited the Israeli Parliament when it occupied its makeshift premises on King George V Street in Jerusalem. I lost no time in inspecting the new premises when it moved to its huge pink pagoda on a hill on the outskirts of West Jerusalem. However, apart from a brief spell in the public gallery, listening to a dull debate, I had not spent much time there. Now, on successive days, I was going to visit two members of the Knesset, said to be on the far right and the extreme left, and try to get the hang of their views.

My friend Benny had come down to Jerusalem from his kibbutz. By now he had four sons, and the oldest, whom I had seen grow up from babyhood, had fought in Lebanon and been in Beirut. Benny had abandoned his work in the kibbutz for the duration of my visit, in order to drive me where I needed to go and interpret for me when this assistance was required.

We drove up the hill in the late afternoon and parked outside the huge gate. At this gate there was a kind of quarantine block, where visitors could be filtered through security checks. I used to feel superior to the Israelis because of the tight security they felt it necessary to maintain, compared to the much more casual attitude in Britain. But no-one had ever been murdered in the Israeli Knesset, whereas Airey Neave was assassinated within the premises of the House of Commons as recently as 1979. I could not help a smile, though, at the name of the vetting machine. It was called FRISKEM.

Conscious of our virtue in having been given clearance by FRISKEM, we made our way across the ceremonial pathway up to the Knesset building itself. A sensational sunset was exploding over Jerusalem. The city's skyline was enchanting in silhouette. A crescent moon and one star were pasted on to the evening sky.

Another set of security guards passed us into the building, and we were directed to the office of the Tehiya Party, the National Renaissance Party, on the fifth floor. I was going to meet Rafael Eitan, known to everyone in Israel simply as 'Raful'.

Raful had retired as Chief of Staff a couple of years previously, and been elected to Parliament as a representative of this small right-wing group fifteen months after that. I had read a certain amount about him, and I did not find it encouraging.

In the *Jerusalem Post* I noticed an item about an encounter that Raful had had with a journalist. This reporter had asked him to confirm that he had made a certain statement before the Foreign Affairs and Defence Committee of the Knesset. The proceedings of such committees are highly confidential, and it is an offence to reveal what goes on in them without proper authorization. All the same, it is the business of journalists to get hold of leaks if they can.

Raful barked at the reporter: 'Who told you what I said in the committee?'

The journalist, very properly, refused to reveal his source. At which Raful exploded: 'If it were up to me I would have you arrested, thrown into prison, and questioned. I would interrogate you myself until you broke'.

It was he who had been Chief of Staff at the time of the appalling massacre at the Sabra and Shatilla Palestinian refugee camps in Lebanon in September 1982. The Israeli Government had set up an inquiry into this massacre, under the chairmanship of Yitzhak Kahan, the President of the Supreme Court. This report revealed chilling attitudes among senior Israeli ministers and army officers. Because of its frankness, its lucid and dispassionate appraisal of the abominable events it examined, the Kahan Report was also a glorious testimonial to Israeli democracy at its very best. The report had criticized Raful severely, possibly more severely than anyone else upon whom it commented: 'We find that the Chief of Staff did not consider the danger of acts of vengeance and bloodshed being perpetrated against the population of the refugee camps in Beirut; he did not order the adoption of the appropriate steps to avoid this danger; and his failure to do so is tantamount to a breach of duty that was incumbent upon the Chief of Staff.'

So this was the Raful I was about to meet, the same Raful who was on record as having said, 'There is a military solution to the problem of the PLO.'

When I had told people that I was going to interview this man, they laughed in a jeering sort of way. One person pondered, 'I wonder if he will speak to you in English or Hebrew? In English he has a vocabulary of two hundred words. In Hebrew it is better, five hundred words.'

Another politician, quite senior, told me a story about when Raful, not yet Chief of Staff, but still a high-ranking army officer, had been responsible for the Litani operation, a limited anti-PLO offensive into Lebanon. Menachem Begin was Prime Minister at the time, and Cyrus Vance, the American Secretary of State, was visiting Israel. Begin instructed Raful to explain to his important visitor what had taken place during this military action. Raful asked permission to speak in Hebrew, but Begin insisted that the description be provided in English as a courtesy to their guest. Raful pondered a moment and then told his story in full: 'We come. We kill. We go.' Now I was about to meet this alarming man.

On the fifth floor of the Knesset we wandered around a claustrophobic corridor, peeping round doors to see if we had come to the right room. The place was a hive of small offices, since it seemed that each party was allotted its own premises and there were, after all, fifteen parties in the current Knesset. None of them had won enough seats to form a government, or even a coalition. So the two largest parties, Labour and Likud, bitterly opposed to each other though they were, had reluctantly agreed to join together in a national unity administration, with the bizarre arrangement of a Premiership alternating between the two. At length we came to the Tehiya office. There was an ante-room, filled with hangers-on doing nothing in particular. Eitan was not yet ready for us and, while we were waiting, one of the more purposeful hangers-on showed me, with some pride, a framed statement on a wall in which Raful had committed himself not to accept a Parliamentary salary. This sounded pretty noble, but of course the statement did not say whether he received any kind of pension as an ex-Chief-of-Staff.

Now I was ushered in. There he was, Raful. He was a thickset man, quite small. He had steel-grey hair and bulging eyes. He seemed to be gazing at me suspiciously, but it might just have been those eyes. He was wearing a blue short-sleeved shirt, under which I could see a khaki under-vest. He looked very military.

We sat down. The Foreign Office had sent along a nice man to interpret, and Raful indicated that he prefered to speak in Hebrew. I asked Raful about his party, the Tehiya-Tzomet alliance. Tehiya, my Foreign Office explanatory briefing had told me, meant Renewal. Tzomet stood for Crossroads.

'This is an ideological movement,' replied the general. 'Our central idea is to put life into the Zionist movement. To get a response from young people.'

I knew that Raful was regarded as a territorial expansionist, so I asked him what he regarded as his country's borders.

He replied, 'Eretz Israel, the Land of Israel, consists of the British Mandate borders plus the Golan Heights. The Golan Heights are to be kept as a punishment for the Syrians. And that means Jews living everywhere within those borders.'

I listened to him, but I was not looking at his face. I was distracted by a curious mannerism. He had taken off his watch. He had carefully folded the metal strap so that the watch sat on the strap. Now, with his right hand, whose middle finger I saw was scarred, he was spinning his watch round and round on the axis of the folded strap. He did this over and over again. He did not stop. He reminded me, irresistibly, of Humphrey Bogart as Captain Queeg in the film of *The Caine Mutiny*.

Now, in businesslike military fashion, he was telling me what he and his party were all about. He said that he had four national goals, with five principles to guide implementation, and based on three preferences. This all seemed complicated to me, and to avoid getting muddled I decided to take it all down carefully in tabular form.

Raful's four goals
1. To remove the threat of the elimination of the state.
2. To have a society which would attract people from outside.
3. To reduce economic dependency.
4. To strive to achieve recognition of Israel's borders and the people's rights within them. (I gathered he meant the Jewish people here, even though there are hundreds of thousands of Arab Israelis.)

Raful's five principles
1. Settling the land
2. *Aliyah* (immigration of Jews)
3. Education
4. Work as a supreme value
5. Readiness to struggle for all these things.

Raful's three preferences
1. Security
2. Education
3. Settlement and *aliyah*.

Well, that was it; but where did all those hundreds of thousands of Arabs fit in, Israeli Arabs within the old borders and West Bank Arabs who would live inside Raful's new expanded borders?

'They will all be Jordanian citizens,' said Raful confidently. 'They will be Jordanian citizens resident in Israel, foreign residents. They will not be Israeli citizens.'

I was a bit baffled about this. What if Jordan did not want to have them as citizens? What about the large number of Arabs in the Gaza Strip which, under Raful's regime, would not be Israeli citizens but who had no possible claim to Jordanian citizenship?

It did not appear that Raful had thought about this one. He seemed nonplussed for a moment. Then, 'I don't know about Gaza,' he conceded, adding, and taking the concession away immediately, 'but they will not be Israeli citizens.'

We then got bogged down in a discussion about the status of these people who were to lose their citizenship. Would they have to pay taxes?

'Yes, their tax duties will be the same as any other alien living in a foreign country.'

I pointed out that these aliens in other countries to whom he referred became aliens by coming from somewhere else to the land where they would be aliens. His aliens would become aliens by staying put in their homes. It did not seem fair.

I went on to ask about their chances of stopping being aliens and becoming citizens. Could they apply for citizenship by satisfying certain conditions like, say, Israelis living in the United States?

'They could *apply*,' said Raful.

But would there be any point in their applying? The general's lack of any response made his position clear. He was perfectly ready to make comparisons with foreign nationals resident in other countries when they were to his argument's advantgage, but not otherwise.

There did not seem much more to be got out of our conversation, and I was just about to make my polite farewells when Raful stopped spinning his watch and brusquely indicated that the interview was over. I was being dismissed. Whether he would have wished to interrogate me until I broke, I could not say, but I had a feeling that he would have liked to put me on at least a minor charge.

Next day I was back at the Knesset, this time to see someone very different. This was Shulamit Aloni, who was a left-wing member, regarded by some as an extremist. I had read how, at a demonstration by religious zealots against Sabbath opening of cinemas in Tel Aviv, she had been denounced by screamed taunts of 'Whore, whore' and 'Abomination'. Ms Aloni had been a member of the Labour Party, had indeed been Minister without Portfolio in the government led by Yitzhak Rabin which had been defeated by Begin in the 1977 election. Since then, however, she had left Labour and formed her own Citizens' Rights Movement, known in Hebrew as Ratz. She was a lawyer and fifty-six years old. I was due to see her at 2 p.m.

There I was, then, at just before two, walking along the same corridor on the fifth floor of the Knesset building, peeping through doors and trying to find the Ratz office.

I found it. It had a little sticker on the door, rather nice, with the Ratz name in Hebrew, and a tree growing out of it. I went in. There was a pretty teenage girl, and no-one else. She did not know when Shulamit Aloni was coming back, had never heard of me, and, indeed, was simply someone's daughter who just happened to be sitting there, charming as she was. I went away, made some phone calls, returned; still there was only the girl, still she knew nothing about anything. I went to the Labour Party office and sat there for some minutes. I was about to abandon the appointment when a message arrived that Ms Aloni was on her way.

I accordingly returned to her office, where the teenage girl had been joined by a much smaller girl, who was busily crayoning something. As I stood there, Shulamit Aloni hurtled in.

She was a tall woman with frizzy blond hair. She was dressed in a brown blouse and a long patterned skirt which emphasized her height. She wore a huge, heavy necklace and a studded brown belt. She was breathless. She apologized. She had got the time of our meeting wrong. Had I had anything to eat? I sighed, though comfortably. I was back with the Left, where I belonged and to which I was accustomed. This was the disorganized Left, never on time, who could so easily be out-manoeuvred by the people like Raful who were always on time.

Yes, I had had something to eat, I said. Ms Aloni sank, breathless, on to a bench by the window in this cluttered little office with the teenage girl and the crayoning child. She beckoned me to sit next to her. She immediately began to smoke.

I started my interrogation.

'What has gone wrong?' I asked.

'Everything,' she replied, encouragingly. 'I'd be glad if we could start everything from the beginning.' She spoke in fluent English.

What she was bothered about was theocracy or, to put it another way, theocratic justification of autocracy.

'The Nazis', she said, 'used Wagner because he created the necessary mythology for a thousand-year Reich. In the same way Begin used the Bible to justify his theory of the Holy Land as a place for the redemption of the Jewish people – and for eternity.'

Begin, she went on, offered a further justification: 'We are the victims of the Holocaust and the victims can do no wrong. So we have a right to destroy Arabs.'

She then turned on the Labour leaders who had governed Israel for nearly thirty years from 1948 to 1977. 'They never tried to educate Israelis in liberal humanitarian ideas,' she claimed. 'Such humanistic ideas as exist here derive from the Common Law and the British Mandate. Labour adopted a Bolshevik system using bureaucracy to bestow patronage.'

I listened to this woman as she spoke, earnestly, passionately, maybe a little too humourlessly. An extremist? It seemed to me that she could fit quite easily into the British Labour Party, and not the left of the spectrum at that. Indeed, pretty well everything she had said to me would have been perfectly acceptable to British Liberals.

Now, she went on, the Right in Israel had been trying a new way of governing. Recently she had read out to some university students a speech that Mussolini had made, and she had asked her audience to guess who had spoken these words. Some said Begin, others suggested Geulah Cohen, a fellow-member of Eitan's parliamentary grouping, who had just announced her intention to campaign for the introduction of the death penalty for terrorist murderers.

I tried to pin down Shulamit Aloni. She said everything

had gone wrong. But what was the everything? Was it the division between Ashkenazis, the Jews who derived from Western, Central and Eastern Europe (and the United States), and the Sephardis, stemming from the lands of North Africa, Asia and parts of Southern Europe?

She impatiently brushed aside my suggestion. 'I'm not worried about that,' she said. 'Intermarriage will solve it in time.'

So what was she worried about? 'The main problem is the Jewish Established State.'

The rabbis wanted to keep the purity – I gathered she meant racial purity – of the people. 'They are changing a democratic modern state into a Mecca or Vatican of the Jewish people.'

She blamed Labour. 'The Labour Party has never been sensitive to genuine human rights. Now we have a Khomeinistic theocracy.'

She sounded glum. But she did not sound beaten. 'We haven't yet passed the turning point,' she pronounced. 'We have got to start in the schools, we have got to fight in the schools.' Funny; she was so unlike Raful in every other way, but she agreed with him that the schools were where the future of Israel would be decided.

'The problem is', she said, 'that young people who support the Right join the Right. Young people who support the Left leave the country.'

She got up from the bench, went to a shelf, and took down a sheaf of leaflets. 'Here,' she said, 'maybe you would like to read these.' I promised I would study them.

As I too rose, I asked her if she would be voting in favour of removing parliamentary immunity from an extremist member of the Knesset, Rabbi Meir Kahane. They would be debating the issue in a few days' time.

She grimaced. 'Yes,' she said. 'But I don't like it. I don't like having a debate, The Knesset versus Kahane. I don't like a Kahane Festival.'

I then went to one of the Knesset cafeterias. Unlike a second cafeteria farther along the same floor, this was a restricted place. Only members of the Knesset and other privileged persons were allowed in. As we entered, there were certainly quite a few Knesset members, including several I knew and waved to. There were also a very great many privileged persons, journalists, and the kind of political groupies who hang around every Parliament building in every country in the world that has a Parliament.

It was lively and noisy, but it was pleasant. The tables were all decorated with neat blue cloths. As I looked around, I felt that something was missing but could not put my finger on it.

Then I realized. In Britain or the United States, Members of Parliament or Congressmen would be entertaining constituents who had come to visit their representative. Here, there were no constituents. The proportional representation system in Israel, based on a national list, meant that Knesset members did not have constituents. They represented everyone in general but no-one in particular.

I sat down with Elazar Granot. I had peeped at his biography in a useful list provided by the Foreign Office and had seen that he was fifty-seven years old. He looked considerably older than his years, as did Raful Eitan. Perhaps it was because of the lives of stress these people led in this turbulent country.

Granot, whom I had met once in London, was a member of Mapam, the Marxist party which had fought many elections with Labour as part of the Alignment but had now split off in opposition to the coalition with Likud. He also reminded me that he was a kibbutznik, and shyly mentioned that he was a poet too. There was something agreeably bashful about this man. He was terribly polite, almost innocent. Innocence, I had found, was a characteristic, generally attractive, sometimes irritating, of members of Mapam. He was a big fellow dressed completely in green, green open-necked shirt, green cardigan over it. He offered me some coffee and I reciprocated by cross-questioning him.

He was full of complaints about the Labour Party and insisted that the Alignment was over for good and all. Mapam's future, he was sure, lay with Shulamit Aloni and the Peace Now movement, possibly with other minor group-ings. Peace Now had been formed in 1978 to exert pressure on Begin to persist in negotiations with Egypt, and had been especially active following the invasion of Lebanon in 1982.

The Left, he said, had to get back to campaigning, in the streets and in the factories. He told me that he had recently been to a factory and had a meal in its canteen. The experience had been reviving, he assured me.

I had to remember that, unlike in Britain, socialist politi-cians in Israel did not necessarily have regular contacts with factory workers or indeed with city dwellers. Granot himself, though born in Jerusalem, lived on a kibbutz, and the strength of Mapam lay in the rural kibbutzim, eighty-four of which were allied with the party.

Elazar gently told me that he was an optimist and then added, contradicting himself, 'It's going to be worse.' He was not at all concerned about the ethnic divide, which he believed would pass. But he too was deeply worried about theocratic extremism, particularly in the army, and feared that chauvinistic and fundamentalistic ideas – his English was very good, if a little stilted – were gaining ground, es-pecially among the young.

'The Labour Party', he said, 'must come back to education.' Here it was again, I thought. Everyone believed that educa-tion was the key.

'There must be a new youth movement,' he insisted. 'Face-to-face meetings are essential. The history of the Labour movement must be taught.'

I parted from this civilized, decent man who, like Shulamit Aloni if less aggressively, believed in the power of reason.

I returned to the Sonesta Hotel and there I studied the documents that Ms Aloni had given to me. They were attrac-tively produced, decorated with the Ratz movement's perky little tree. They were clearly, if solemnly, written, and I was particularly interested in having a look at the Platform of the Ratz movement, to see just what extremist policies these people were advocating.

They wanted to establish 'the security, freedom, welfare,

and quality of life of the individual and citizen as central to society and the State'. Well, that seemed all right.

I read on. Freedom of conscience and religion for each individual and community. Prevention of religious coercion. The right to raise a family without limitations deriving from ethnic origin or religion. For the Arab citizen, equality of opportunity and the elimination of discrimination in the political, social, economic, and legal spheres.

By now I was puzzled. What was extremist about such policies? Maybe the rest of the document would make things clear.

Curbing inflation. Full and creative employment. Advancement of the underprivileged sectors. Rooting out of bribery and corruption. Raising the level of education among all strata and sectors of the population. Encouragement of basic and applied research. A lasting peace with Israel's neighbours including the Palestinians.

These were not revolutionary policies. To an outsider, they were amiable clichés. Yet Ms Aloni and her three colleagues in the Knesset were regarded by many as leftist trouble-makers. I knew another of these four, Mordechai Bar-On. He had helped me with some research several years ago, when he was Chief Education Officer of the Israel Defence Forces. A less provocative person would be difficult to find.

Now he was dubbed a left-wing trouble-maker, alongside the formidable but perfectly conventional Shulamit Aloni. What had happened to Israel, created by socialist pioneers, that people like this were now either detested or humoured as fringe politicians? What had happened to Israel that Raful, a man who had been censured in the most stringent terms by a Commission whose chairman was the President of the Supreme Court, could be elected to Parliament within eighteen months of that censure instead of retiring into a corner to hide himself? What had happened to Israel that Raful's Tehiya could in an election win nearly twice as many votes as Ms Aloni's Ratz, and indeed become the third strongest party in the state?

3

The Maimonides Manifesto

What was really going on in this schizophrenic land? I felt
I had to find out. But before I obtained opinions, I wanted
facts. I made enquiries. I was told that the person who could
really give me the information I needed was someone called
Dr Sarah Shemer. Dr Shemer was not only the most famous
pollster in Israel, she was also the most successful. I had
been shown a story in the *Jerusalem Post* headed POLLSTER
SCORES BULL'S-EYE. It was about the July 1984 Parliamentary
election.

The item began: 'One pollster who calculated it right with
amazing accuracy was Dr Sarah Shemer, who in this campaign conducted polls on behalf of the Likud. In mid-July
she projected 45 Knesset seats for Labour and 40 for the
Likud, stressing that the gap might possibly narrow a bit
further. Her findings were challenged by Labour's pollster,
Dr Avi Diskin, who insisted that a 16-seat gap continued
to exist in Labour's favour. Even on election day, he continued to predict 50 seats for Labour and 37 for the Likud.'

In fact, on election day, 23 July, the result was Labour
44, Likud 41. I decided that I had better meet this Dr
Shemer.

Someone gave me a telephone number, and I telephoned.
A woman answered. It was Dr Shemer herself. I asked her
if we could meet to discuss electoral, sociological and ethnic
statistics. She agreed right away, but suggested we leave our
appointment for a few days so that she could collect the
necessary material.

Accordingly, we arranged for me to telephone again on a given morning, to her office number, at the Palace Hotel, Hayarkon Street, Tel Aviv. On the appointed day, I made my call, as agreed. 'Dr Shemer, please.'

A strident female voice asserted, with what sounded like considerable satisfaction: 'No-one with that name works here.'

I was bewildered. I had previously spoken to Dr Shemer on that very number. 'But she told me to telephone her.'

There was silence, followed by a click, followed by another silence. Then, a different, but equally strident, female voice.

I said again, 'Dr Shemer, please.'

'She will not be in for another hour.'

I had come to Tel Aviv especially to meet Dr Shemer, so I made up my mind not to telephone again, but simply to go to this Palace Hotel.

I walked northwards along Hayarkon Street, a dismal thoroughfare at its southerly end but, farther into the outskirts of Tel Aviv, turning itself into quite a classy boulevard beside the sea. At length I saw the Palace Hotel. Once I was inside, the hotel, despite its name, looked seedy. I was directed to Dr Shemer's room. I went in. It was empty; of people, that is. It was full of papers and books piled untidily on a desk. I wondered what to do next.

There then hurtled into this room an extraordinary young woman. She had brown hair as frizzy as Ms Aloni's. She had blood-red lips. She was wearing a man's shirt over which she had on a multicolour striped sweater, adorned with a vermilion scarf. She wore pink slacks. Over these were fitted woollen leg-mittens, and tall leather boots. On her arm was a huge red plastic bangle. On her ears were large, blue plastic discs, circular in shape. She looked as though she was in her early twenties. I learned later that she was born in 1951.

I was about to open my mouth to make enquiries, or even apologize, when this remarkable person spoke. 'I am sorry to have kept you waiting,' she said breathlessly, in American-accented English. 'They told me you had telephoned.' There could be no doubt about it. This was the legendary pollster, Dr Shemer herself.

She threw down a bulging plastic carrier bag, seated herself behind the desk and beckoned me to take a chair.

'What can I do for you?' she enquired. I reminded her that she had promised to bring some statistical material for me.

She seemed at an utter loss. She thought for a moment. 'I haven't been able to get it together yet,' she said.

This Dr Shemer seemed to me to be not only the most glamorous pollster in the business but also the most disorganized. Yet the *Jerusalem Post* had said she was the best.

I was in despair. 'I shall be leaving the country soon,' I wailed.

She took pity on me. 'I will send it to you in England,' she soothed. 'Meanwhile, have a look at my essay in this book. It contains all that you really need to know. The figures are for 1981, but nothing has changed much.'

She took out of a briefcase, which I had not previously noticed, a book called *The Roots of Begin's Success*. For a moment I thought she was going to give me it, but she showed no sign whatever of doing so, even returning the book to the briefcase right away in order to make the situation absolutely clear.

'I'll get hold of it in England,' I said. 'Meanwhile, do you mind if I ask you some questions?'

'Not at all.'

'What are the factors governing election results in Israel?'

Dr Shemer took out a packet of king-sized cigarettes. She lit one and puffed at it expertly.

'Well,' she said, 'it is the ethnic mix that is shaping events. In Israel 70 per cent of the Labour votes are Ashkenazis and 70 per cent of the Likud votes are Sephardi.'

'Why is that?'

'The Ashkenazi Jews are the ones who have been making the decisions. The Labour Party has not opened up positions for Sephardis. The Sephardis have been told by the Ashkenazis how to act, how to speak, how to behave. And they've had it.'

I asked, 'So what does this mean electorally?'

'At present the Ashkenazi-Sephardi divide in the electorate

is fifty-fifty. But the Likud is running with the wind. Labour is running against the wind. The Likud becomes stronger by three per cent every four years.'

I thought of Shulamit Aloni's placid view that time would solve the problem, and enquired: 'But what about inter-marriage and education? Surely they will slow down the move to the Likud?'

'They will have a counter-effect, but we cannot quantify it. Still, the fact is that the Sephardis have a lot of hang-ups about their position in Israeli society. The Sephardis perceive Labour as a very élitist party. If the Labour Party is to have a chance of reversing the trend, it has to take off its tuxedo image.'

That was as much as I could get out of her. Our conversation concluded and we parted with the utmost cordiality, Dr Shemer promising me faithfully that she would send me further material.

The material, in fact, never arrived, so after my return to England I went to the House of Commons library and asked them to get me the book, *The Roots of Begin's Success*, that Dr Shemer had recommended. They did not have it in stock, but borrowed it from the Foreign Office library. I read it with care. Much of it was tedious and, to me, irrelevant. Dr Shemer's own essay, however, was extremely informative, and so were two others, one by Avraham Diskin (possibly, I speculated, the Avi Diskin over whom Dr Shemer had triumphed in forecasting the election result) and another by Amiram Gonen, Professor of Geography at the Hebrew University in Jerusalem.

The main points they made were as follows:

Israel is struggling towards a two-party system.
In the past, Labour had been by far the dominant party, with lots of minority parties jockeying for position. In the 1984 election, 15 parties had gained representation in the Knesset, but the two major blocs, Labour and Likud, hold almost all the power and compete for support from the minor parties to form coalition governments they can dominate.

The major institutions of the state of Israel were created by Ashkenazis.

They include, for example, the trade union movement, the political parties, the armed forces and the kibbutzim.

While the Labour Party was very much dominant, it enjoyed widespread support among the Sephardi immigrants.

There were several reasons for this. Most Sephardis had grown up in cultures which encouraged attitudes of political passiveness and acceptance of the authority of the existing leadership. Since, in addition, the major immigrations of Sephardis were later than those of Ashkenazis, this often led to lack of confidence and grudging acceptance of Ashkenazi dominance in the earlier years of the state.

The Labour Party was also dominant in governmental and administrative organizations which dealt with employment, housing and social services. This meant that the electorate, and particularly the lower strata – in which much of the Sephardi population was concentrated – was directly dependent on Labour-run organizations.

More recently, Sephardis have shown a strong tendency to support the Likud.

As immigration has increased the number and proportion of Sephardi voters, particularly from African countries, and as earlier Sephardi immigrants have become more confident, this change became a factor of the very first importance in Israeli politics. In the 1977 election, the Likud won enough seats to form a government for the first time. In 1981, despite a pronounced overall swing to Labour, the long-term trend was even clearer.

Diskin provided statistics which showed that, in the 1981 election, Labour had increased its vote by 12.5 per cent. Yet in four affluent Ashkenazi areas in Jerusalem, Tel Aviv and Haifa, its increases ranged from 17.1 per cent to 26.7 per cent. In three out of four of these districts, the Likud vote actually fell. On the other hand, in that same election in four poor Sephardi districts in those same three cities, the Labour vote recovered by at most 7.4 per cent and as little as 0.8 per cent, failing to recoup huge declines in the 1977 election. Even those changes, however, were less startling – according to Professor Gonen – than the comparatively sharp increase in support for the Likud in the new development towns, predominantly inhabited by Sephardis. Labour had been outpaced by the Likud ever since 1965 in the old inner urban neighbourhoods. The Likud's predominance then spread in 1969 to immigrant housing developments on the outskirts of the old cities, to new immigrant towns in inner Israel, and by 1977 to the development towns on the periphery of the country.

How can we explain this crucial ethnic split? Direct Sephardi dependence on Labour and Labour-controlled organizations has decreased. This is partly because upward social and economic mobility has weakened the dependence of poor Sephardi residents of housing estates, new cities and towns on social-service provision. Meanwhile, many governmental and administrative organizations engaged in the allocation of resources have been streamlined, so that the less well-off are dependent, if at all, not on discretionary Labour-run organizations but on benefits provided as of right to everyone impartially. It is hardly surprising, therefore, that Sephardis have felt much freer to express their political convictions at the polls; but why have they swung so strongly towards Likud? Important factors include the following:

* revelations of corruption led to a decline in the prestige of the Labour establishment

* the Labour establishment is perceived as serving the needs of the Ashkenazi population; voting for the Likud can therefore be seen as a sort of ethnic protest

* the Labour Alignment is also perceived as serving the interests of the upper and middle classes

* Sephardi political culture is almost certainly more attracted to strong and charismatic leadership; this was provided by Labour's long-standing leader, David Ben-Gurion, in the past, but his mantle was taken over by the leader of the Likud, Menachem Begin

* the Sephardi population are said to be more religiously inclined and thus more sympathetic to the religious gestures

of major components of the Likud such as Herut
* the Sephardis tend to have a more hawkish attitude to
Arab-Israeli relations, a position closer to the position of
Likud than the Alignment

*The party division in the country is more and more the same
as the ethnic division.*
Between 1977 and 1981, the Likud vote had gone from being
60 per cent Sephardi to being 70 per cent Sephardi. Even
more striking, the Ashkenazi component of the Labour vote
had risen from 61 to 75 per cent.

*Obvious demographic trends make the future look very bleak
for the Labour Party.*
In the 1981 election, support for Labour was strongest among
immigrants from Europe, next among Israeli-born children
of European immigrants and then among children of native-
born Israelis. Likud support was strongest, on the other hand,
among Israeli-born children of immigrants from Asian, African and Arab countries, and next strongest among such immigrants themselves.
   Between 1980 and 1995, the groups among whom Labour
support was strongest will have declined from 50 to 39 per
cent of the population; the two strongest Likud groups will
have increased from 45 to 49 per cent. At the start of the
1980s the two main blocs were level-pegging. By 1995, the
Likud will have an enormous advantage over Labour of 7
per cent – an absolutely crushing lead under Israel's system
of proportional representation. In each election, this lead is
likely to increase by 2 per cent. (When I met her in person,
Dr Shemer quoted a figure of *3* per cent, whether in error
or as a result of further research.) The implications for the
future of the Labour Party are as obvious as they are depressing.

   This was information that I obtained after leaving Israel.
When I was still there, my failure with Dr Shemer compelled
me to look to alternative sources of information.
   I had been told of a fascinating symposium on the 1984

election which had taken place at Tel Aviv University. The contribution of Professor Ephraim Ya'ar, Director of the University's Institute of Social Research, had, it seemed, been especially illuminating. I managed to get hold of a copy of what Professor Ya'ar had said, and it was indeed remarkable.

The professor declared that 'The outcome of the recent elections reflected the definite trend to the Right that has been going on now for approximately fifteen years.' The ethnic changes noted by Dr Shemer and others were linked to this rightward swing: 'You have to make a distinction between the initial drift towards the Likud – which first gave a sign as early as 1969 and later manifested itself on a larger scale in 1977 and 1981 – and the identification with the Likud in the years thereafter. The initial vote for the Likud was a protest vote: the Likud was the only alternative whereby youths of Sephardic origin could register their protest. It wasn't the Likud ideology that attracted them, it was feelings of deprivation that pushed them in this direction. If, for instance, the Right had been in power during the early years of the state, then the exact opposite would have happened – feelings of deprivation would have pushed these youths into the arms of the Left . . . In the aftermath of the possibly one-time protest by young people who voted Likud in '73, an imprinting process was initiated, and the disposition toward the Likud became a major emotional tie. In order to put a halt to it, something drastic must occur.'

A new kind of religious ideology in the life of Israel had also developed at about the same time, as the result of the occupation of the West Bank – Judea and Samaria – in 1967: 'The situation that emerged in Israel after 1967 gave the religious sector ideological substance for waging a struggle. And the militance of religious ideology is far less flexible than that of secularist ideology. If, for instance, according to proponents of the security argument, the occupied territories are not an end unto themselves but a means to protect the state, then in religious ideology, the very control over the territories became a sacred end unto itself.'

So the two trends came together – the switch to the Right and the new brand of religious dogma – to produce a novel development: 'The reality that emerged in post-'67 Israel reinforced right-wing ideology. Because youths by their very nature tend to be more idealistic, and in their idealism more radical than their parents, and because no competing ideology had emerged in Israeli society, it's no wonder that a sizeable proportion of the youth drifted toward the only available ideology – national or nationalist ideology.'

Labour had become less ideological, less able to offer an idealistic alternative to young people. The Right offered an exciting substitute. The contrast was pointed by another participant in the symposium, Professor Yohanan Peres, of Tel Aviv University's Sociology and Anthropology Department. 'The Labour Alignment comes across to youth as responsible, experienced and elderly. The Likud has a fresh and youthful image, less tied up with property. Paradoxically, it is the Israeli Right that has a fresh, dynamic, and appealing image . . . I see a universal connection between phenomena such as Khomeinism, the Moral Majority in the U.S., and the growing drift towards Tehiya – the party of Rafael Eitan – and Rabbi Kahane. This phenomenon takes on a different expression and form in every country. It's very interesting to compare what's happening here with the Khomeinistic phenomenon in Iran. The style, of course, is different, but both developments belong to a single wave.'

These analyses from sober academics were disturbing, and I decided to go and talk to a man who, I had been told, thought about such issues as profoundly as anyone in the country. He was Dr Moshe Lissak, Professor of Sociology at the Hebrew University of Jerusalem. So I crossed Jerusalem to Mount Scopus, where that university is situated.

It took me a long time to find Dr Lissak's room in this exceptionally hideous and labyrinthine collection of buildings, built in the years since 1967 when the Israelis captured East Jerusalem. When I got there at last, it was minute and cramped, scantily furnished, with piles of journals, untidily stacked books and file boxes taking up much of the limited space. Professor Lissak himself imperturbably accepted my apologies for being late, not being in any way surprised that visitors should get lost. He was a small, gnomelike man wearing heavy glasses and dressed in an open-necked shirt and slacks.

I told the professor that I was interested in learning about social, ethnic, ideological and electoral trends.

'I have a ten-hour course on that,' he said, mildly but meaningfully.

I indicated that I did not have that much time available, and asked him to explain what he could during the hour or so that he could spare me.

Professor Lissak began by agreeing with Dr Shemer that there had been no great change in the voting patterns since 1981, so that an analysis based on 1981 was still largely relevant. He confirmed the ethnic voting pattern that Dr Shemer had outlined. He was able, though, to provide further enlightenment about the prognosis for the future which was, if anything, even more discouraging for the Labour Party. Dr Shemer had been unable to offer any projections about the effect of inter-marriage between Ashkenazis and Sephardis. Professor Lissak was somewhat better informed: 'The inter-marriage rate at present is roughly 20 to 21 per cent,' he said. 'It is increasing at a rate of one half to one per cent.'

I asked him if he could indicate what happened to electoral allegiance as a result of inter-marriage. He said he could not, but went on: 'There is a difference of political support within the Sephardis. The Iraqis, for example, are more inclined to Labour than the North Africans. The North Africans vote Likud in a very high proportion of 80 per cent. And the North Africans are inter-marrying less than the others. It is a matter of class.' So the Sephardis who were giving the Likud its biggest boost were the Sephardis whose ethnic pattern was most likely to remain intact.

Even within classes, though, the Sephardis were different from the Ashkenazis: 'There is an enormous Oriental middle class in terms of income, but not in terms of educational and occupational prestige. A quarter of the Orientals are self-employed.

'There is no difference of income between Ashkenazis and Orientals in the middle class. In fact, the income gap is narrowing. But the education gap is not narrowing.

'It is true that there has been a big increase in the number of Orientals at university. Thirty years ago there were hardly any. Now 21 per cent of the relevant age group are receiving a university education.'

Still, however, this was less than the Ashkenazis; and there was another significant difference: 'The gap between the Ashkenazis and the Orientals is growing in terms of occupational prestige, because much greater educational qualifications are required for the more sophisticated industries.'

So even at the top level the Sephardis were going to continue to lag behind the Ashkenazis. And lower down? 'The Labour Party has never succeeded in mobilizing the Oriental working class. It has had some success in mobilizing them in trade unions. But it has not motivated them ideologically. They did not join the party and they did not join the kibbutzim. The idea of being part of a collective beyond the ethnic family or the ethnic family group is a strange concept to them'.

I asked Proffessor Lissak why, then, the Sephardis had gone on voting Labour for so long. I wanted to learn whether he shared the views on this matter put forward by his fellow academics: 'After 1948, 70 to 80 per cent of them voted for the Labour Party as led by Ben-Gurion, partly because he was seen as the Redeemer, partly because of their dependence on the absorption machinery.

'The problem was that the Labour Party wanted speedily to integrate them into existing Israeli society, out of their traditional culture. This meant changing relationships between fathers and children, between men and women. The effect was traumatic.

'The Ashkenazis, the veterans and their sons, had taken over the leading roles in all major sections of the community. There was a First Israel, the Ashkenazis, and a Second Israel, the Sephardis. The division between the two became a real factor in the 1950s and the 1960s. It was a geographical division, too. The Sephardis were sent out to the periphery of the country.

'The Ashkenazi frontiersmen of the 1920s and the 1930s

were regarded as pioneers and heroes. That isn't the case with the Sephardi frontiersmen of today. They attract no social regard.'

I asked Professor Lissak at what point the Sephardis had felt free to break away from the Labour Establishment: 'It was under Levi Eshkol, when he succeeded Ben-Gurion as Prime Minister in 1963. He devolved responsibility from the centre. He opened up the system. So the minorities, as they were then, became much more independent. The Herut Party, in particular, exploited that independence, trading on the legitimacy that Eshkol had given to the opposition parties.' Herut, Begin's party, was the dominant grouping in the Likud.

'So', Lissak went on, 'the Second Israel became much more exposed to new ideas. They realized what the gaps in society were. They also realized their power. They became much more open to the appeal of other parties and their support for the non-Establishment parties grew.'

I was being given a potted version of a ten-hour academic course, and it was both impressive and convincing. Professor Lissak continued by stressing Sephardi attitudes to tradition, religion and Arabs: 'The Sephardis have a psychological suspicion of Arabs. They compete with them occupationally. And there are the historical memories among those who suffered from the Arabs in the lands they came from.'

From what the professor was telling me, the implications for Labour's future were as grim as foretold by Dr Shemer and her colleagues: 'The Orientals are now 60-40 in the 18-20 age-group. In roughly the 18-25 group, support for Kahane, Tehiya and the Likud has a much higher proportion than in the population in general.'

What is more, these trends were being strengthened by what had been taking place in army education: 'There has been a failure to educate the army in democracy. Eitan as Chief of Staff opened up the army educational system to rightists and fanatics. Rabbis now have an important educational role in the army. In the 1950s and 1960s you never saw a rabbi in army ceremonies. Now they're always there, and those who complete training get a Bible.'

I asked Lissak if the religious question was really important. 'Theocratization is a fundamental issue. It is a powerful
element ideologically, and exerts a gravitational pull to the
extreme Right and more orthodox patterns. The Oriental
Jews did not use to be part of the orthodox religious establishment. Now there is Shas, the oriental religious party of the
new orthodoxy. It is unrelated to Zionism. It is far more
fanatical.'

I thanked Professor Lissak, left his little cell, and, trying
to avoid falling over some cleaners who were mopping down
the dim and seemingly endless corridors in this ugly, oppressive place, I made my way out of the university and into
the sunshine.

I was brooding. Repeatedly – first by Shulamit Aloni, then
by the academics – I was being warned about the baneful
effect of this new growth of religious fanaticism. I decided
I had better find out something more detailed about it. So
I made enquiries and was supplied with a copy of a lecture
delivered not long before by a Professor Uriel Tal. It was
called 'The Foundations of Political Messianism.' It looked
heavy, even turgid, stuff; but I forced myself to read through
it carefully and was glad that I did. This lecture was both
brilliant and alarming.

It argued that the sharp, practical, almost ruthless realism
which had dictated the policies of the state of Israel for nearly
forty years was in danger of being ousted by a mystical national megalomania. This merged practical policies with heady
visions, and was just as ruthless as before, if not more so.
Phantasms were hovering over the land, and were being called
as witnesses to testify about what its boundaries should be
and who ought to live within those boundaries. Religious
messianism insisted that returning one handful of earth to
the Arabs would lead to a doom presided over by the Devil.
As I read, I could certainly understand what Professor Peres
had meant when he compared fundamentalist fanaticism in
Israel with Khomeinism in Iran. Mystical ideas were not
simply to be employed for spiritual inspiration. Rather, they
were being headily expounded in order to lay down a practical
political and military schedule intended to be implemented

by the Israeli government. The argument, though complex, was perfectly clear.

It stemmed, explained Professor Tal, from the acceptance of 'the total sacredness which applies to every clod of earth and grain of dust on which our feet tread.' This conviction led to the assertion that 'every place in the Holy Land on which a Jew treads is holy.' Historical symbols were to be transformed into political facts. Holiness was believed to reside not in man nor in his spirit, but in Place; and Place meant not something symbolic and amiable, 'but rather physical localities, such as trees and stones, graves and walls.' Now this primitive worship of boulders and rocks was literally to be turned into national doctrine, and the arguments supporting this doctrine, and forcing it upon the government of the country, were to be found not in ministerial statements or state documents but in rabbinical exegesis. Tal had even tracked down the relevant text. He quoted it as follows: 'The primary source used for this approach is Mitzva 4 in Nachmanides' interpretation of Maimonides' enumeration of the positive commandments. Nachmanides writes: "We were commanded to take possession of the land given by the Lord to our forefathers, to Abraham, Isaac and Jacob, and we will not leave it to the other nations. And He said unto them (Numbers 33:53): 'You must take possession of the land and settle there, for to you I have given the land to occupy.' "

The boundaries of the land were set out in another passage, Deuteronomy 1:7, according to Nachmanides. Predictably, they are very broad, extending into Lebanon and to the Euphrates (now in Iraq); nonetheless, the Jews were to occupy the whole area, 'lest you yield from any place.'

Why, I asked myself as I read on, should anyone concern himself with such gerontological ramblings? It might provide fun, even excitement, for a coven of bearded, elderly obsessives mumbling to themselves over yellowing texts in small, dusty garrets in hidden parts of Jerusalem; nobody else, surely, was going to take such stuff seriously. The very next section of Tal's lecture sharply disposed of any illusions I might have had. For he now revealed that these views had the support of the Chief Rabbinate of the state of Israel, an authority not only supremely powerful in religious matters but possessing the ability strongly to influence government policy. The rabbinate had issued rulings concerning the holiness of the Occupied Territories and of Israel's political sovereignty over them, and had proclaimed a religious duty which was to be put into effect by political action. Said Tal: 'The Chief Rabbinate's decision of 22nd Adar 5736 (1977), for example, states the following:"The Temple Mount is Mount Moriah, the site of the Temple and of the Holy of Holies, the place where the Lord G–d of Israel chose to house His Name, which was sanctified by ten holy blessings by David, King of Israel: the Jewish People's right to the Temple Mount and the site of the Temple is an external and inalienable divine right, over which there can be no concessions". In the light of this sacredness there is no room for any compromise: neither with regard to Time (i.e. concessions at least for the time being, for a year or a generation) nor with regard to Place.'

This was inflammatory stuff. Not only was Temple Mount, to which the rabbinate asserted an 'eternal and inalienable right', inside annexed East Jerusalem. It was surmounted by two mosques which were among the holiest places in Islam and which, by the logic of the rabbinate, would have to be removed or erased. Sadly, as I was later to discover, even though the Israeli government had not so far been persuaded, there were individuals who certainly had been and were ready to act in accordance with the rabbinate's ruling. In a way they could be pardoned for being influenced. After all, here was the central religious authority of the state of Israel laying down a policy of no concessions on withdrawal from occupied lands, basing its political stance on Maimonides as interpreted by Nachmanides.

A more general decision in 1980 forbade the transfer of *any* land in Israel to the gentiles, *including the territory conceded to Egypt in return for peace*, because it would mean violating a commandment in the Covenant of Abraham: 'thou shalt not show mercy unto them' (Deuteronomy 7:2). Even arguments based on the traditional concern for the saving of life were not to be used to justify giving gentiles the right of encampment within the borders of Israel.

Professor Tal went on to rub in the meaning of what he had said so far. He stressed, mercilessly, the significance of the statements, ancient and (much more disturbing) modern, which he had pieced together: 'As we have seen, we are neither talking about a band of crazy prophets, nor about an extreme minority on the fringe of society, but about a dogmatic schoool of thought and methodical doctrine which inevitably leads to a policy which cannot tolerate the concept of human and civil rights, because this absolute perception of the dimensions of Time and Place is incompatible with the concept of tolerance.'

The professor then listed the available policy options of those who put forward these views. There were three, increasingly frightening, which set out how the Jews of Israel should deal with the human and civil rights of non-Jews who were unfortunate enough to be domiciled either in Israel or in territories conquered in war by Israel.

The first of these, said Tal, was still 'relatively moderate'. It stated that the equality of human and civil rights was nothing but an alien European democratic notion which was directly at odds with the Jewish presence in the Holy Land. Accordingly, the principle of human rights had no validity in Israel, and must be irrelevant to the attitude of the dominant Jews to their Arab fellow-inhabitants of the country. The status of Arabs in Israel, therefore, could only be that of aliens. This was, of course, precisely the policy which had been put forward to me by Raful Eitan.

The second was much worse, but also had its ardent adherents. This declared that human rights for Arabs were simply not possible because the existence of the Jews in Israel was not compatible with the presence of Arabs there. Consequently, achievement of a truly Jewish Israel depended on the emigration of Arabs. That this was a profoundly provocative proposal was admitted by one religious magazine which, in advocating it, sternly warned: 'As the issue would shock the public at the moment, one should try to refrain from explicitly talking about the expulsion of the Arabs as a temporary measure, yet the principal attitude is that there is no place for Arabs in the country.'

The last of the options listed by Professor Tal was quite simply monstrous: 'The third position concerning the question of the non-Jews' human rights is based upon a positive commandment from the Torah – the wiping out of any trace of Amalek; i.e., actual genocide.'

This 'solution' – a tragic word for Jews to use when talking of the intended obliteration of another people – was expressed in an article by a Rabbi Hess, published in the student journal of Bar Ilan University in Tel Aviv, a religiously dominated seat of learning of the utmost respectability within the Israeli educational system. The article was entitled 'The Commandment of Genocide in the Torah'. Apart from a few members of a fringe religious group, no-one, said Tal, was known within the rabbinical community to have dissented from this school of thought. What is more, before my travels in Israel were over, I was to find at any rate one reverend gentleman who was prepared openly to advocate it.

I read on and on, depressed and dismayed, through pages citing a series of obscure references. Professor Tal's conclusion, however, could not have been more explicit: 'One can therefore sum up and say that this is a political form of Messianism in which the individual, the people and the land are united organically under protection of absolute holiness. It is based on a metaphysical perception of political reality which is expressed by an absolute perception of Time and Place. The danger of this totalistic outlook lies in its leading to a totalitarian perception of political reality – because it neither leaves time nor place for the preservation of the non-Jew's human and civil rights.'

During these days of discussion and exploration, my conversations and my reading had made clear to me some of the ethnic, social, structural, political, ideological and religious clashes that were bedevilling Israeli society. I felt that now I had better go out into Israel and look at how these ideas fitted into, or conflicted with, life as it was actually being lived.

4

Interlude with a
Demonstrative Rabbi

I went to Hebron, the second largest city on the occupied
West Bank, to buy some of the famous turquoise and sub-
marine-blue glassware. I then decided to go into the centre
of the city, which I had not visited since 1967, when the
West Bank towns had become accessible to visitors to Israel
following the Six-Day War. Even then I had been warned
that Hebron had a tradition of turbulence, that there had
been a gruesome massacre of Jews forty years before, and
that to enter the mysterious Casbah might not be safe. I
had, however, gone into the Casbah and had found it neither
dangerous nor mysterious, just another fairly messy bit of
a characteristically Arab town.

Now, however, I did find something nasty and threatening
about Hebron. Partly this was because the people who lived
there were notorious for being highly nationalistic and xeno-
phobic. I experienced their hostility for myself: when I made
as if to photograph an elderly bearded man buying the chick-
pea confection felafel at a street stall, I was sharply warned
by another man not to do so. Children called derisively after
me in the street. When I wandered into a series of dark
passages, I felt quite unsafe and was glad to emerge unscathed
into an open square.

Partly, though, the atmosphere of tension was the result
of a deliberate decision by ultra-religious Jews to establish
themselves in Hebron, asserting their right to settle near
to the alleged site of the tomb of the Biblical patriarchs.
The monument was claimed for themselves by both Muslims

and Jews in a competition of stridency in which both sides could more than hold their own. Evidence of the Jewish presence was obvious, almost obtrusive. There was a large souvenir shop containing the kind of rubbish that was available anywhere in Israel proper, but different from souvenir shops in Israel proper in that it was barred and shuttered for protection against throwers of stones or hand-grenades. Almost next to the Casbah itself was the synagogue, a partly constructed edifice which was protected by Israeli soldiers who only permitted access to those who could demonstrate their bona fides. I looked in for a moment, but found it as disappointingly unimpressive as most synagogues in Israel apart from the little gems in the hilltop city of Safad in Galilee. Next to the synagogue was a ramshackle building which was, I was told, the home of Rabbi Levinger, the head of the Jewish community of Hebron and a man who, as a provocation, made a habit of promenading through the Casbah; however, the Arabs disappointed him by allowing him to make his progress unharmed. I would quite have liked to meet this notorious Rabbi, but was told he was not at home, being away on one of the demonstrations on which he apparently spent a good deal of his time. Suddenly I had had enough of Hebron. I would not have been surprised if a grenade had at any moment whistled through the air (as indeed one had only a few days before) and I did not want to stay and take the risk. I was hungry, but had been warned that while the Arab felafel on sale in the town tasted fine, it might upset my stomach. I decided to go to Jerusalem and find something to eat.

So we bowled along, on a lovely winter day under a clear blue sky, through an undulating countryside with, from time to time, hilltops crowned with the red roofs of Jewish settlements. Since it was Friday, I was anxious to get to Jerusalem before the capital closed down for the Jewish Sabbath. We were making pretty good progress, and Bethlehem was in sight ahead of us, when Benny suddenly brought the car to a halt. At first I though that something had gone wrong with the engine; but then Benny pointed to the other side of the road.

We had arrived at the notorious Dehaishe refugee camp for Palestinians. Across from this collection of grubby, tumbledown buildings was a kind of nook gouged out of the bank on the side of the road. Inside this nook were slouched two rather grimy and unkempt young soldiers, holding menacing-looking guns but otherwise appearing far from menacing, indeed dejected almost to the point of bursting into tears. Next to them was standing what appeared to be an animated scarecrow. This personage was dressed in an open-necked shirt, over which were placed in turn a grubby pullover and an even grubbier khaki jacket with a hood attached. He wore, in addition, a pair of shapeless trousers and sturdy but battered shoes. On his head was perched a little wool cap. His face was decorated with an untidy beard, basically ginger in colour but tinged with grey. I looked at him with astonishment as he made his way across the road to join us, followed by another, smaller man, clearly a hanger-on. 'That', said Benny, 'is Rabbi Levinger.'

I was astounded. I had always thought of a rabbi as a figure of authority, dressed in a long black coat and wearing a black hat, immaculate and, according to temperament, either benevolent or threatening but above all dignified. Those were the rabbis I knew in England, those were the rabbis I had seen in Israel, marching around Mea Shearim in Jerusalem with the air of proprietorship. It was almost impossible to fit this scrawny figure into that context of rabbidom, particularly as, now that he approached much nearer, I could see that his spectacles were coated with dirt, and his teeth — as he flashed a welcoming smile at me — were even browner than his complexion. This was sunburnt and windblown, no doubt from exposure to the weather during countless demonstrations. Yet here was, indeed, the fabled Rabbi Levinger, who for years had been linked by rumour and speculation with the Jewish terrorist underground on the West Bank.

The most notorious terrorist organization called itself Terror Against Terror and, since the word 'Against' is translated into Hebrew as *Neged*, they were known by the initials TNT, entirely appropriate considering the explosives that they were notorious for planting and, indeed, setting off. I had been given a leaflet apparently issued by these murderers and mutilators. It had been alleged to me that this leaflet was in fact a forgery issued by Arabs to discredit the West Bank settlers. However, its contents certainly fitted in with the undeniable facts I had learned about the TNT movement.

There was no printer's imprint. The heading was simply: JEWISH ACTION: TERROR AGAINST TERROR. Flying alongside it was a drawing of the Israeli flag. The text ran, furiously: 'At a time when the real heroes of Zion are being held in Israeli prisons and condemned by Israeli judges the patriotic organization TERROR AGAINST TERROR warns those traitors among the Jews that endanger the security of the Jewish State by their activities.'

It continued in paragraph after paragraph of sustained invective: 'Israel is undergoing a crisis brought about by the cowardice of the politicians who have yielded under the pressure brought to the international scene by Arab tycoons and their stooges on the European and American continents. These corrupt leaders of both the political groupings in our country are tampering with the fate of the Jewish nation casting doubt on the accomplishments Jews have won in their incessant fight against their Arab enemies. They have unleashed psychical terror against the heroes who have refused to stand idle while the Arab enemies have made themselves at home on the soil promised to the Jews by G–d. This terror can meet with no other response but equal terror.'

Having thus impartially condemned every conventional politician in the country from Shimon Peres and Yitzhak Rabin to Menahem Begin and Ariel Sharon, the aggressively right-wing former Defence Minister, the authors of the leaflet went on: 'These corrupt leaders are trying to impose such moral values on the consciousness of the Jewish nation that are in contradiction to the heritage of Zion. They pass heroes for criminals! They protect the enemies from the just wrath of their victims! TERROR AGAINST TERROR shall not allow these traitors to act as representatives of the Jewish State. We rebuff the government of disgrace even if it describes itself proudly as a "government of national unity." '

The organizers of TNT set themselves specific tasks: 'We will free the heroes prosecuted unjustly in Jerusalem. We have enough strength and power to do it. Other fighters have replaced those that have been arrested and they shall deliver their heroes from prison bringing their fight for the expulsion of the Arabs from the Holy Land to a close with success. They shall succeed in burning out the evil from our midst.

'We are not afraid of any casualties. For one casualty on our side there shall be two casualties on the side of the enemy and his associates. Our principle is not "an eye for an eye" but "two eyes for an eye!" '

The leaflet concluded, in determined vein: 'Death on the Jewish traitors and their associates!' Its final words, however, were quite merry: 'Hurray for the heroes of Zion!'

That there have been terrorist acts by Jews is undoubted. There is, however, controversy, even confusion, about exactly how these heroes of Zion are organized. Israeli police, investigating their allegedly patriotic but frequently lethal activities, detected at least three independent groups, possibly more, responsible for terrorist outbreaks over a period of several years. The title Terror Against Terror was apparently used indiscriminately by several different cells, some seeking out targets among Christian sects accused of missionary work among Jews, others more conventionally and expectedly aiming at Arabs. The 'underground', as it became known, was formed as early as 1978, although its first really notorious activities did not begin until 1980. I set out to find out what I could about these activities and obtained a great deal of information, especially from the archives of the *Jerusalem Post*.

Whether there was a central command or a group of separate gangs, what was undoubted was the destructive and lethal effect of the terrorists' exploits. This was not surprising, since most Israeli males have at one time or another served in the armed forces and are familiar with weapons. Furthermore, there are weapon depots all over the country, ready to be raided. One arms cache that was discovered consisted, alarmingly, of: four Kalashnikov rifles; nine M-16 rifles; 14

grenades; five Uzi submachine guns; two telescopic sights; one sharpshooter's rifle; three pistols; one silencer for an Uzi; 87 rounds of specially silenced Uzi ammunition; one magnesium grenade; 35 sticks of plastic explosive; 13 rifle-propelled grenades; 113 M-46 mines; 10 various demolition charges; 104 explosive bricks weighing 111 kilos.

Armed in this formidable manner, the Jewish terrorists got to work. The following incidents are noteworthy:

April 1980: the windows of 70 houses and 120 cars belonging to West Bank Arabs in Ramallah and nearby Al-Bireh are smashed.

Late spring 1980: five bombs are prepared to put in the cars of prominent Arabs – including the Mayors of Nablus, Ramallah and Al-Bireh – all vocal PLO supporters. Three are placed as planned and two explode as planned. One mayor loses his legs, another a foot; the third calls a bomb-disposal expert, who loses his eyesight.

1982: an arson attack on the Baptist Church in Jerusalem; a bomb attack in a school playground in Hebron.

January 1983: Jewish settlers fire shots from a passing ambulance at a kindergarten in Nablus and a bus parked beside it.

February 1983: a booby-trapped bomb explodes outside a mosque in Hebron on Friday (the Moslem day of worship); two people are injured.

February 1983: a booby-trapped grenade injures two boys on a soccer-field in Hebron.

February 1983: a bomb timed to coincide with the end of prayers explodes in an Arab house, again in Hebron; because worship in the mosque had been delayed, the only injuries are to a four-year-old girl. Jewish settlers from nearby Kiryat Arba are responsible.

July 1983: masked terrorists attack the Islamic University in Hebron with automatic rifles and a grenade, killing three people and injuring 33.

December 1983: an eleven-year-old girl shot dead in Nablus; several attacks on Arab targets in Jerusalem: a Series 26 grenade – property of the Israel Defence Forces (IDF) – explodes in Salah a-Din Street, the main shopping thoroughfare in East Jerusalem.

December 1983: two grenades are found on the steps of the Franciscan monastery on Mount Zion, one at the Greek Orthodox seminary; another is found lashed to a doorhandle at the Dormition Abbey, yet another near the mosque in Beit Safafa. A police spokesman describes all five grenades as 'professionally placed', 'with something about it reminiscent of IDF training'.

January 1984: a guard outside a mosque in Hebron is injured when a booby-trapped grenade explodes on a Friday morning; later, another grenade causes damage at another Hebron mosque.

March 1984: a nun is almost killed by a grenade at the White Russian Orthodox convent at Gorney in Ein Kerem near Jerusalem.

April 1984: masked assailants attack a bus carrying Arab workers from Ramallah.

April 1984: assailants steal mines from a dump on the Golan Heights and take them to the Jewish settlement of Kiryat Arba, just outside Hebron. They are fitted with mines and placed in buses in various suburbs in East Jerusalem.

It was this last attempt, an attempt which failed, which led to the discovery of some of those responsible and to a trial which began in Jerusalem in May 1984 and which turned out to be one of the longest and most divisive trials ever held in the state of Israel. The district detective responsible for the arrests said that the group consisted of 'fanatic religious Jews'. At least one of them, however, appeared in court dressed in an army uniform with captain's rank.

The most alarming evidence that emerged during the trial related to what, if it had succeeded, would have been an act of terrorism that might have precipitated an international conflict: an act of terrorism whose would-be perpetrators might have deluded themselves into believing that they were carrying out an edict of the Chief Rabbinate, as described in Professor Tal's lecture. This was a plan to blow up the Dome of the Rock, one of the holiest places in the Muslim world, situated directly on top of where the Jewish Temple used to be sited. The motives of the would be participants in this manic act of terrorism varied. Some of those involved were dominated by a deep, mystical belief that the Temple Mount should be restored to Jewish hands as a prelude to the construction of the Third Temple. Others, more mundanely, hoped that an attack on such a scale on so emotionally significant a target would be enough to put a stop to the peace process with Egypt and halt the withdrawal from Sinai. Still others wanted some kind of 'revenge', and others still were crudely anti-Arab racists.

The evidence against all of them revealed commitment and efficiency. They set themselves up in a highly structured organization. A carefully organized expedition was sent to the Golan Heights, where contacts at an IDF base helped them steal explosives from a weapons plant. These explosives were stored at a *moshav* – a co-operative settlement – on the Heights. Elsewhere, in a workshop in Israel itself, specially designed containers were manufactured. Eventually, some thirty separate charges of explosives were prepared and secreted in various parts of the country. All this preparation was, however, in vain. The plotters never got round to carrying out their project.

One of the earliest to be sentenced at the Jerusalem trial was a young man, Gilad Peli, who came from another *moshav*, Keshet, on the Golan. He pleaded guilty to a charge of membership of a terrorist organization and to three counts of conspiracy to commit a crime, the illegal transport and possession of weapons, and damage to army property. He was involved in the planned attack on the Dome of the Rock, and the assaults on the leaders of the Palestine National Guidance Committee. He also took part in dismantling and stealing explosives from a weapons system called Viper and the transport of no fewer than fifty Syrian mines, from which were manufactured the bombs that were planted on the five Arab-owned buses.

Much to the consternation of his family and friends, Peli was sentenced to ten years' imprisonment, plus another five years to be served concurrently. Passing sentence, Judge Israel Weiner of the Jerusalem District Court declared: 'The mere existence of a terrorist organization is enough to undermine and rock the basis on which a democratic government is founded.' Others, however, were not so certain. A Likud Member of Parliament, Meir Cohen-Avidov, who at the time was a Deputy Speaker of the Knesset, said of those on trial: 'These boys are the pride of Israel. They are the best. We should be proud of them.' An opinion poll showed that, while 71.9 per cent of the Israeli electorate opposed the creation of a Jewish group to fight terror with terror, 18.7 per cent favoured the idea. Among Likud supporters, no fewer than 26.2 per cent supported the TNT group.

One of the most outspoken supporters was Rabbi Levinger. He stated, firmly: 'If Arabs can murder Jews, Jews can steal weapons to fight back.' Indeed, many of the leading figures in the underground had come under Levinger's influence. Four of the defendants in the trial of terrorists were all with Levinger in his early days of struggle to return to Hebron. For Levinger, although he looked ridiculous and behaved ridiculously, was a dangerous man. He was, indeed, the man who began the political settlement of the West Bank, and it was he who laid down the strategy for that settlement.

Moshe Halevi Levinger was born in Jerusalem in 1935, a child of parents who had immigrated from Germany. He was sickly as an infant and spent a good deal of time in a Swiss sanatorium. He was educated at religious seminaries and spent his obligatory military service not on patrol, as he claimed, but at ultra-Orthodox kibbutzim. He lived on a kibbutz, working as a shepherd and a rabbi; but eventually he left. His wife, who bore him eleven children, could not stand the life.

Levinger did not fight in the Six-Day War but, shortly after it ended, visited Hebron. 'My visit stirred up a storm in me that did not abate for weeks,' he said. He was determined to settle there, and made his move on the eve of the Passover in 1968. It was a propitious time for him. Moshe Dayan, the Defence Minister, was in hospital after being seriously injured in an archeological dig. Shlomo Gazit, the co-ordinator of operations in the Occupied Territories, was in mourning for his father, a time of seclusion for Jews. So those who might have stopped him were out of the way.

Levinger booked rooms at the Park Hotel in Hebron. He told the owner, Fahd Kwasmeh, that he wanted to hold a *Seder*, the ritual meal celebrated on the eve of Passover. The proprietor agreed, not suspecting that his new guests did not intend to leave. Levinger successfully resisted the attempts of the authorities to remove him. Whenever the army made a move to evict him, he made sure television cameras were present and adorned himself in a prayer shawl, thus resembling the popular conception of a rabbi and making it impossible for him to be taken away by force.

He stayed, first in the Park Hotel, then impertinently moving into the military government building, where he set up what he called a *yeshiva*, a religious seminary, but what was in reality simply a place where settlers could squat. Because the building itself, a military camp and prison, was unsuitable for children, structures for the settlers were built in the courtyard. From these beginnings came the decision, achieved by Levinger by wily manipulation of the political process, to build the settlement of Kiryat Arba outside Hebron.

Yet it was Hebron itself upon which Levinger had his eye, a town holy to Jews as to Muslims. When in 1976 there were Arab demonstrations in the town, Levinger sent in his supporters armed with submachine guns and rifles. They refused to lay down their arms when so instructed by soldiers. They set dogs on the rightful inhabitants. Levinger was tried by a military court, and acquitted. During the inquiries into the Jewish terrorist ring, he was held for eleven days for questioning, but was eventually released. The evidence against him was not strong enough. The state attorney's office could not risk an unsuccessful trial: 'If we were to prosecute and lose there'd be a terrible stink.' Yet the police were convinced that Levinger did have knowledge of the underground's activities.

This, then, was the apparently absurd man whom I met by the roadside. He spoke mildly enough to me, but he had said to others on another occasion that 'eventually the entire nation will understand' the activities of the terrorist network. He had a grin on his face when I met him, yet he had been absolutely serious when he said that the terror network was 'a new affair, like the settlement movement, which in the beginning was controversial,' but that the members of the underground were 'righteous activists' whose motives 'eventually the entire nation will understand'. This lone demonstrator outside Dehaishe, with his one ridiculous follower, had been described as 'possessing an outstanding ability to lead'.

So there he stood, where he had already been stationed for two months. He was well equipped, with food, water, cooking utensils, a spirit stove, and a tin bench to sit on.

'What are you up to?' I asked him.

'I am demonstrating against stone-throwers.'

I suggested that if he was not stationed there so provocatively no-one would throw any stones.

'Every Jew must have the right to go anywhere in Israel without being afraid of being molested', he retorted.

I told him that he was not, at the moment, in the state of Israel. He was in no way disconcerted: 'My principle applies to all the territory for which Israel is responsible', he explained.

Unlike more stubborn but less intelligent zealots, Levinger did not go into the question of what was Israel and what was not.

Rabbi Levinger's lone groupie now intervened. I asked him his name and he told me it was Shlomo. He informed me, somewhat improbably, that he had been born in Stamford Hill, in London.

'Have I a good English accent?' he asked hopefully.

'You speak English badly,' I responded with some honesty. He seemed quite disappointed and indeed appeared somewhat forlorn, a small, dark-haired, unshaven figure, unkempt, perhaps, in emulation of his mentor. He too, however, was no fool. When I went across the road to question the soldiers about their assignment of protecting this pair, he called across to them not to respond. They, obediently or truthfully, indicated that they could not speak English and, by now rather irritated with the whole episode, I did not bother to get Benny to come and call their bluff by offering to interpret.

My absence seeking to converse with the military deprived

me of being able to listen to an encounter that now took place between Rabbi Levinger and the local Arab *mukhtar* who at that moment happened to stroll by. Benny told me that the *mukhtar*, no fool, confined himself to various innocuous comments about all men being brothers and stone-throwers being crazy.

By the time I got back to the side of the road where the action was, Rabbi Levinger was preoccupied with another topic: 'Guess how old I am,' he tempted me.

When I agreed to essay this conundrum he stood straight and tall like a child being told to be at attention. I thought. 'You are fifty years old,' I said.

'No, you are forty-eight,' said Benny.

The rabbi seemed rather pleased. 'I am forty-nine,' he revealed. He then turned to me: 'Why don't you join my demonstration?' he suggested.

'No. What you are doing is nonsense.'

The rabbi appeared in no way put out. As I left, he was applying himself to the literature he had brought along to while away the time and, no doubt, to afford some relief from Shlomo's devoted but not entirely stimulating company. He had with him two books, the Bible and a volume about the geography of the Lebanon.

Cars coming along the road from Jerusalem paused when their occupants spotted the rabbi. People leaned out of their windows and waved encouragingly.

To me Rabbi Levinger was a pernicious clown. To the Israeli authorities he was a dangerous rabble-rouser, with whose cunning antics they had for nearly twenty years been quite unable to cope. To far too many Israelis he was a patriot fighting for a cause – a chauvinistic and fanatical cause – which they either believed in implicitly or at any rate regarded with good-natured toleration. My encounter with Rabbi Levinger, almost surrealist though it had been, was a sour taste produced by an ulcer in the stomach of Israel.

5

The Kahane Festival

I was back in Jerusalem and at the Knesset again. This time I was going to listen to a debate. Actually, since my knowledge of Hebrew is nowhere near good enough for me to follow with confidence a collection of complicated speeches, I was going to do the best I could while I was there; Benny had the job of sitting beside me, whispering explanations to me whenever he could get away with it, and taking notes which he would translate to me afterwards.

The reason why I wanted to attend the debate was because it was about Rabbi Meir Kahane. It was, in fact, the Kahane festival that Shulamit Aloni had told me, a few days before, that she dreaded. The Knesset was going to discuss whether to take away part of the rabbi's parliamentary immunity, and I thought it would be instructive to watch the Israeli democratic system operating under extreme stress.

The Knesset chamber was pretty impressive. There were bare stone walls, relieved only by a picture of Theodor Herzl, the founding father of Israel. I had been told that Raful Eitan had, upon being elected five months before, demanded that a flag of the state of Israel be installed in the chamber, and had even offered, as an amateur carpenter, to supply the pole himself. A decision to place the flag in the chamber had been made, but it was not there yet.

At the front, under Herzl's picture, was the dais, on which was situated the chair of the Speaker (in the centre) with places for advisers on either side. To the Speaker's right was the rostrum, from which members addressed the Knesset as if it was a public meeting rather than, as in Britain, speaking from wherever they happened to sit. Below the dais were the individual seats of the members (not benches as at Westminster), one for each of the 120 excluding the Speaker. They were placed in a semi-circle, and, like the chairs on the dais, were covered in a dignified muted brown material. It was probably leather, though I suppose it could have been some kind of plastic.

Each member had his or her own desk, and on each desk was the member's name, a bulging brown folder, and a blotter. There was an individual microphone for each desk. The seats were arranged in concentric tiers, the innermost tier reserved for members of the Government. Placed at the front of the chamber, to the Speaker's left, was a big box. This was a ballot box; today the Knesset was going to employ a rare, special procedure of voting by written ballot to decide whether to infringe a colleague's immunity.

At 4 p.m. prompt the Speaker strolled in, with no ceremony of any kind. He just arrived. To my astonishment he was formally garbed, even to the extent of wearing a tie; he did not, however, wear any special form of ceremonial dress. After a brief pause he struck his desk three times with a hammer, and the session was in progress, by my watch a minute late. By the time of this official commencement, about twenty members were present. Many of them, in the old Israeli tradition, wore open-necked shirts; but quite a lot, like the Speaker, had ties around their necks. An Arab member was particularly neatly dressed. I noticed Kahane. He had come in unobtrusively and was sitting in a back row seat to the centre-right of the Speaker. He wore a jacket, as befitting a rabbi, but an open-necked shirt, as befitting an Israeli. He had on a skull cap and was studying a volume that might have been either a Bible or a prayer book.

A ginger-haired person, with an equally ginger beard, rising from the Likud section, went to the rostrum. Benny told me that his name was Micha Raiser, and I looked him up in the list of members of the Knesset which the Foreign Office had thoughtfully supplied to me. He was 38, I read, born in Tel Aviv, married with three children. This man was chairman of the Knesset's House Committee, and it was his job now to explain what was going to happen. The Knesset was going to be asked to deprive Meir Kahane of the freedom of movement granted by Article 9(a) of the Knesset Members' Immunity Law.

Members of the Knesset have all kinds of immunities that protect them from arrest or interference, whether inside or outside the Parliament building. Article 9(a) states that no order prohibiting or restricting access to any place in the country that is not in the private domain shall apply to Knesset members, unless the reason for the order is state security or military secrecy. Kahane had been using this immunity to go to places where Arabs lived or worked, and causing commotions of an unacceptable kind. If the Knesset removed that immunity, the police in future would have the right to put a stop to Kahane's provocative trouble-making just as they could with any other citizen.

Raiser, speaking with the monotony that I was soon to learn was quite customary in this place, said that the House Committee had decided to make this recommendation by twelve votes to eight. They were not happy about the proposal, and he himself had not voted for it. All the same, that was the recommendation, and it was unprecedented. Up to now, a member's immunity had only been removed upon the advice of the Government's legal counsellor. This was the first time ever that the Knesset itself was going to do it, on its own initiative. Still, he said, despite the split committee vote he knew of no other issue that had united the Knesset as had this one: 'No political body, from Tehiya (Eitan's very right-wing party) to the Communists, has concealed its dissociation and even disgust.' He meant disgust at the way Kahane carried on.

Raiser then left the rostrum, and the Speaker delivered a homily. This Speaker was called Shlomo Hillel. He had been born in Iraq and served in a previous Labour Government as Minister of Police; a thin, hawk-faced man, he said he wanted the members to understand their responsibilities.

'This', he declared, 'is not an easy day for the Knesset. Great emotions are involved.'

He appealed to members to conduct the debate in a calm way, and he announced the ground rules. Kahane himself would be allotted fifteen minutes to put his case. All other speakers would get five minutes each. There was, he said, a great demand to speak. Already thirty members had notified him of their wish to catch his eye.

The gallery was filling nicely now, and so was the chamber. By 4.15 p.m. fifty members were there, and Benny told me that this was a very high attendance. Now Kahane was called to address the Knesset, and positively bounced up to the rostrum. He spoke in a quiet, unexcited way, reading from a prepared text. Even I, with my limited understanding of what he said, could hear that he was both skilled and vicious. His speech seemed to irritate or upset Shulamit Aloni, who throughout moved restlessly about the chamber, an imposing tall figure in her long brown dress.

The Rabbi referred to himself throughout in the third person as 'Kahane', and pronounced Arab names with obvious contempt. He said that it was not his mouth that the Knesset sought to close, but that of Judaism. Zionism had meant this country to be one with a Jewish majority, but what he called the 'terror of the Left' was so strong that people were afraid to utter the word 'Arab' for fear of being regarded as racists.

At this point Kahane broke into a diatribe. He warned the Knesset against the SS. Forty years after the end of the Second World War, this seemed rather a gratuitous admonition. However, the two letters 'S' turned out to stand not for evil Germans but for two members of that very Knesset, Yossi Sarid and Edna Solodar.

Sarid, I knew, was a left-wing Labour member who had been an early campaigner against the war in Lebanon and who, rather than support the Peres-Shamir National Unity Government, had left Labour and joined Shulamit Aloni's Citizens' Rights Movement. Edna Solodar I had already met. She was a tiny woman, seemingly inoffensive and not particularly radical, who came from the kibbutzim and was now the Labour whip. It seemed exceptionally far-fetched to compare either of these two with Nazis, but, of course, being exceptionally far-fetched was Kahane's style.

Anyhow, Sarid was even more dangerous than poor Edna, it seemed. Kahane vehemently demanded that Saridism be removed. He told Likud members darkly that Sarid was really after them. He, Kahane, was first. They would come next.

The Speaker was getting restless. He interrupted to advise Kahane that he had only one minute left out of his allotted fifteen. Kahane brushed aside the intervention, and ranted on: 'If the Knesset votes against me today,' Kahane promised, 'I'll continue to do my job. But Miari and Toubi will be the victors.' I checked with my list of members. Both of these foes were Arabs, Miari representing the People's List for Peace, Toubi the Communists.

A red light flashed, telling Kahane that he had over-run his time; but the rabbi was finishing in his own way, the Speaker shrewdly not cutting off his flow of words.

'I am not afraid,' proclaimed Kahane, with self-conscious heroism. 'I am a Jew, a Zionist. Now you can vote. I am going to pray Mincha.'

Mincha was the regular afternoon prayer and, whether or not he did go off to do that, Kahane immediately left the chamber, to no applause whatsoever.

Now little Edna Solodar stumped up to the rostrum to move the anti-Kahane resolution. She looked quite elderly, though my list of members told me that she was, in fact, only fifty-four years old. She wore a rather drab brown skirt and cardigan.

Edna Solodar did not galvanize her colleagues. Some members chatted quietly among themselves. A young Likud representative idly spun around the empty chair next to his.

Edna did not really have much to say. To carry this motion was the duty of the Knesset, she advised. They must accept their responsibility, she insisted. She left the rostrum after an unremarkable speech which was at any rate highly dignified.

Yossi Sarid, Edna's SS partner, followed his colleague in infamy. He seemed quite an ordinary man, in fact undistinguished in every way. He wore a yellow sweater over an open-necked shirt, and spoke soulfully in a deep voice.

'I prepared a long speech,' he announced. 'But I've thrown it away.' He then got very emotional, not to say sentimental. 'I was called SS,' he said. 'There is a connection between me and the SS.'

He then told an involved story about how, when he was a child of five, his father, who was a great teacher, was asked to go to the Displaced Persons' camps in Germany.

'He said he must discuss something with me. He had been asked to go to Germany to work among the DPs, and he did not think the family's name of Schneider was appropriate.'

'Mr Schneider told his young son that he was thinking of changing the family's name to Sarid, which in Hebrew is spelt in almost the same way as Schneider and means a 'remnant'. And Yossi's father was the only remnant of his family. The rest were lost in the Holocaust.

As I listened to this, helped out by muttered translation by Benny, I though it was sloppy sob-stuff. Yet the rest of the members of the Knesset were listening with rapt attention, demonstrating this by the manner in which they had turned their swivel chairs to face Sarid.

Now Yossi got quite excited: 'Probably not everyone here remembers what Kahane stands for. No marriage with Arabs. No intimate relations with Arabs. Prison sentences for doing so. This reminds me very much of the Nuremberg laws directed against the Jews. It is a terrible thing to see a Nazi Jew.'

The speech's conclusion was certainly grandiose and, so far as I could tell, highly effective. Sarid used the symbol of the Dybbuk, the vexed spirit that can enter a living body and take baneful possession of it: 'I don't know how such a Dybbuk got into us. All I can say is, Dybbuk leave us. Let our souls have peace.'

This was a speech that could only have been made in a Jewish Parliament, and I could certainly see why Sarid got on his opponents' nerves. He effortlessly got on mine, even though I agreed with his sentiments.

Shulamit Aloni had stopped her peregrinations and now, from the floor, attempted a point of order. She asked for the debate to be discontinued. The Speaker said that such a motion was premature. Dr Yosef Burg called out something I could not catch. He was a very venerable member of the National Religious Party, seventy-five years old, who had somehow contrived to hold office in practically every government Israel had ever had. This doughty and persistent survivor was now a Minister without Portfolio.

The debate droned on. The Speaker announced that now thirty-two members had notified him that they wanted to take part.

Next we had a young, rather flabby, Labour member dressed in slacks and a jerkin over an open-necked shirt. Chaim Ramon was thirty-four years old.

Ramon spoke spontaneously: 'If we don't act against Kahane, we are giving legitimacy to what the Nazis did. We are saying what the Nazis did was right, they were only doing it to the wrong people.'

He went on to mention that he had heard that the religious members were not going to vote in the ballot at the end of the debate: 'I call upon the religious people especially to vote and to prove that there is another Judaism.'

I though that Ramon's speech was easily the best so far, but it left his colleagues cold. They paid hardly any attention to him as he declaimed. Yet this was the only genuine oratory I had heard during the past hour.

A little, wizened, elderly man was now called. Benny told me that he was Meir Wilner, the leader of the Communists, and I did not really think I could be bothered listening to him. Other members of the Knesset seemed to share my opinion. His audience was down to only twenty-five.

We decided to leave. Like many eagerly anticipated occasions in the British Parliament, the debate had been something of a let-down. It had been full of abstruse Biblical allusions and references to Jewish literature. The speeches, except for that of Chaim Ramon, had been stilted. Yet this was a Parliament, a real Parliament, a Parliament which took itself and what it did seriously.

As we walked out of the gates, we had to push our way through a throng queuing for the gallery. Mainly the queue consisted of Orthodox Jews, distinctively garbed. Most of them were young, and they seemed somehow dangerous and threatening. They also seemed to be very much in possession.

In the next day's edition of the *Jerusalem Post* I read a report of the remainder of the debate that I had missed. A succession of Likud speakers had opposed the motion.

Meir Cohen-Avidov said that he would not vote for the resolution even though he distanced himself from Kahane's deeds, pronouncements and methods. It was a racist resolution, aimed at Jews, and: 'Kahane is still a Jew.'

Another Likud member, Gideon Gadot, declared that Sarid was the crime and Kahane the punishment, thus putting this rather conventional left-winger and the extremist rabbi on the same level.

When the vote took place, it was carried; but fewer than half the Knesset members had voted for it, even though little Edna Solodar had issued a whip to Labour members to do so. Twelve Likud members did not vote, and, ignoring Chaim Ramon's plea, the religious representatives absented themselves.

It was not very glorious, but it was progress. Kahane, on being informed of the result, made clear that he intended to pay no attention to it, and that he would go the very next day to the Arab village of Taiba; but when he did so, the decision of the Knesset worked. This was the report in the *Jerusalem Post:*

'Meir Kahane was stopped yesterday en route to the Arab village of Taibe. But Kahane said he had achieved his purpose by attracting scores of Israeli and foreign newspapermen to witness the incident.

'Kahane had announced he was going to Taibe after the Knesset vote Tuesday to restrain his movement. Police put up roadblocks and deployed personnel on the roads leading to Taibe.

'Large contingents of journalists came to see Kahane stopped. There were no Taibe villagers or Kahane opponents along the road leading into Taibe, in comparison with the crowds that gathered in August at Umm el Fahm – Kahane's last sortie into an Arab population centre.

'In Taibe, people said they were pleased Kahane had been stopped, and that their confidence in the police had increased.

'But Kahane told journalists afterward that "yesterday I won two Knesset seats, and now I'm getting more".

'Kahane had planned to meet a busload of supporters in the Kfar Sava bus station. But police delayed the bus, saying it had a faulty brake light. Kahane was then told that he would be stopped at a roadblock at Neve Yamin near the Kfar Sava industrial zone.

'At the roadblock, Kahane's yellow-shirted supporters got off their bus, roaring slogans in his praise. Later they tried to hold evening services in the middle of Kfar Sava, but police told them to leave.'

Well, had the action of the Knesset put a brake (whether with a functioning light or not) on Kahane's activities? Or would a backlash of sympathy actually help him, as Kahane himself claimed?

I had already decided that it was necessary for me to meet this man; but how was I to do it? I had asked the Israeli Embassy in London to fix an appointment for me, but they shrank in horror at the very prospect. There was no hope of help from them.

Many of my arrangements were being made for me by my friend Yehiel, the chairman of the World Labour Zionist movement, based in Jerusalem. Yehiel is chubby, and looks innocent. But he is an expert operator and has the additional advantage of being very popular with a wide circle of friends and acquaintances. I had known him for some time, and he had decided to take me under his wing and organize accommodation, meetings and trips for me. Yet even Yehiel, who was ready to do almost anything for me, stopped short at Kahane. It was out of the question for the Labour movement to have anything to do with this man, he insisted. I quite understood, but was still no nearer getting to Kahane.

Then, one day, when I was in the Knesset building, walking through the outer cafeteria, I found my chance. There, sitting at a table, talking to a couple of bearded rabbinical gentlemen, was Kahane himself. Luckily, his conversation was coming to an end. So I simply walked up to him, introduced myself as an English journalist, and said that I would like to have an interview with him.

He agreed instantly, gave me his Jerusalem telephone number and invited me to telephone him any day between 7 and 8 a.m. I took him at his word and a few days later rang him, just after 7 a.m. He answered the telephone instantly, and just as instantly fixed an appointment with me at his party office in Jerusalem at 11 a.m. the following Friday.

It proved almost impossible to find Kahane's office as I battled through the street market in the Machanei Yehuda district, pausing several times to ask directions. At last I reached a bedraggled modern office block. There was nothing on the ground floor, so I climbed a grubby staircase and found myself on a kind of loggia overlooking a central well. I walked along this loggia, examining each window of the shops with which it was lined, and finally saw a woman with a kerchief on her head bustling along with a bunch of papers in her hand. She went into a shop. I peered inside. A lot of photo-copying seemed to be going on. I made inquiries; this was part of Kahane's premises, but not the part I needed. I was directed to another shop front, a few doors along. There it was, a cramped, poky little room. In one wall there was a door behind which, it seemed, Rabbi Kahane was involved in a meeting. No-one in the outer room had the slightest idea that I was coming, but I was told to wait. Sooner or later the rabbi's meeting would end, and then I could see him. The haste had all been for nothing. I learned again that for Israelis appointments are flexible, dates and times are servants, not masters.

This room was untidy, not to say squalid. There were piles of leaflets and posters all over the place. Two men were talking on telephones, in a kind of *obligato* of guttural babble. People were bustling in and out. On a wall was a poster which showed a fist against a star, with the words 'Jewish Defense League of Israel'.

Three boys were sitting at a little table packing leaflets into envelopes. Curiously, despite the assertively religious nature of Rabbi Kahane's activities, not all the males were wearing hats or skullcaps, as observant Jews are supposed to do.

I peeped inquisitively but shamelesssly over the boys' shoulders, to find out what exactly they were doing. What they were at was sending special propaganda leaflets to English-speaking tourists at the hotels: very efficient and rather worrying. Without asking, I simply stole one of the leaflets and took it over into a corner to study. It was both interesting and horrible.

Page one was dedicated to 'Rabbi Meir Kahane. Philosopher! Visionary! Revolutionary! The most different, dynamic, *different* Jewish leader'.

I turned the page. There was a picture of Kahane, looking very thoughtful, quite visionary, I suppose, though not actually all that different. What was printed underneath, under the heading KAHANE IS RIGHT! was, however, very different from anything I had ever read in any Jewish propaganda, however chauvinist, apart from the TNT terrorist leaflet.

It began, arrogantly but not especially unpleasantly: 'The Jewish people is a chosen and holy nation, selected at Sinai to follow the Divine law of Torah.' Some of the policy points that followed were, however, both nasty and paranoid: 'The barring of any intermarried Jew from holding leadership position in the community.' 'Jewish physical defense to crush Jew-haters.' 'Immediate annexation of the liberated land and unlimited Jewish settlement.' 'An end to the threat of an Arab population that will be a majority in Israel by the transfer of Arabs to their lands; the removal of Arabs and their mosques from the Temple Mount.' 'The knowledge that time is short; if not now, there will be no "when".'

The heading to the next page, in large capital letters, read: DEAR JEWISH TOURIST, WELCOME TO ISRAEL! The leaflet then really got down to its message, in which sexual preoccupations took up an unhealthily but significantly large proportion.

'In your brief time here', it said, 'now, allow us to tell you about the things you do NOT hear about in the newspapers or through your tour guides.' What were these secret, suppressed things? Well, one was the revelation that 'the Camp David accord will prove to be a cruel hoax that cost us land, oil, bases and, eventually, many lives... Let us immediately annex all the territories and make them part of Israel.'

Then we began to get to the heart of Kahane's obsessions: 'THE ARAB OF ISRAEL POSES A THREAT TO ISRAEL'S EXISTENCE AS A JEWISH STATE. The Arab of Israel hates the state because it is a Jewish one, that he cannot identify with. His population growth is enormous and he already threatens to turn the Galilee into our Northern Ireland.'

Then sex raised its head explicitly: 'THOUGH IT IS SUPPRESSED there are numerous Arab assaults on and annoyances of Jewish women in Jerusalem. In addition, Israel faces an ironic threat of assimilation in the form of Jewish women living with and marrying Arabs. Israeli women date and bed Arabs, UN soldiers, Portuguese laborers in the Negev and gentile volunteers on kibbutzim.'

Finally, on the last page, was a series of tips for the unwary, headed: JEWISH TOURIST. WHAT CAN YOU DO FOR YOUR PEOPLE AND STATE? FOR YOURSELF?

The advice was wide, even all-embracing: 'Do not enroll in or send your child to a Kibbutz that is non-religious.' 'Beware of the Christian missionaries who cunningly hide behind pro-Israel institutions.' 'Note the anti-religious and anti-nationalist bias of the *Jerusalem Post*. Consider very carefully a paper that is so inimical to the best interests of Israel. Do you subscribe to its overseas edition?'

Then, however, we came to the Rabbi's main preoccupations: 'If you study at a university in Israel, be especially wary. Arabs live with Jews in dormitories and they are – to a person – avid followers of the PLO. Do not date them or have social contact with them. Above all, do not enroll in schools such as Hebrew University, Tel Aviv University or Haifa University, whose policies towards Arabs are tragic.'

Finally we arrived at Rabbi Kahane's favourite horror subject: 'Beware of the young Arab who seeks Jewish women. Often, he tells you he is an Israeli. Ask for his identity card. DO NOT BE ASHAMED. (It can save you terrible grief later on). Do not feel pity for him; he is not oppressed. Date only Jews and do not believe for a moment that the Arab who seems so friendly really loves or respects you.'

As I finished reading this document, ludicrous were it not so vile, Rabbi Kahane's inner door opened. I was about to enter the presence, and I did so with extreme curiosity. Of course I knew about this man. I knew about his disagreeable antics with the extremist Jewish Defence League in America. I had studied with care a transcript of a BBC television programme that had been transmitted not long before; indeed, I had brought it with me to Israel. I had read the brief outline of his life and career in the list of biographies of members of the Knesset supplied to me by the Foreign Office. He was 52 years old, born in the United States, married with three children, lived in Jerusalem.

I had seen him a few months previously on an election programme on Israeli television, and had noted with interest how some of his words had been blotted out, words which contravened election law and had therefore been censored by Israel's vigilant election commission, who had the power to vet all campaigning propaganda before it was transmitted. Now I was to meet him personally. I went into the inner room. A woman, with whom he had been talking, left as I entered. He ushered me to a chair, and I looked around. The office was bare, but somehow messy. On the wall was a chart of planned demonstrations.

I sat down. I saw no point in beating about the bush. So I got right down to it. 'What are your trying to do?' I asked.

Without hesitation Rabbi Kahane replied: 'I'm trying to make this country Jewish. This is a country of Jews. But it is not Jewish.'

I was not at all sure what he meant, so I pressed him to go into detail.

'The only reason to be different is because you have something to be Jewish about. Judaism. Otherwise, you're racist. The left are racist because they are Jewish without believing in Judaism.'

I asked Kahane how he planned to make Israel Jewish.

Once again, his reply came without a moment needed for consideration.

'The Torah shall be the constitution of the country.' The Bible? The Old Testament? This seemed a tall order; however, before I could seek further enlightenment, he went off at a tangent.

'I don't like people who play games,' he declared, ominously. 'This is a country that plays games. This state was created by schizophrenics. The declaration of independence was schizophrenic.'

I took a look at him, as he spoke. He was wearing the same outfit as at the Knesset debate – a sober suit, two-piece, but a shirt without a tie. His hair was thinning. His beard and eyebrows were greying. As he spoke his eyes blinked. He had a nervous tic, a twitch.

He went on: 'Zionism must over-ride democracy.'

He kept making aphoristic statements, extremely provocative in nature and certainly by design. They fitted in very well with the Khomeinistic philosophy described by Professor Tal. Yet I could not get satisfactory explanations of his meaning, although he clearly rejoiced in being frank beyond the point of outrageousness.

'How is the Torah to be the constitution of Israel?' I asked. 'How are books of narrative to be turned into laws governing a country?'

He blinked. He said: 'It will be the Torah as interpreted by the Talmud. By commentaries. By rabbis.'

'By you?'

No reply; but I did not feel I was much mistaken in concluding that the rabbinical interpretation by which Israel was to be governed would be the Bible according to Kahane.

'What are the boundaries of your Israel?'

Once again, the response was prompt: 'The boundaries as given in the Bible.'

'But the Bible is not an atlas. What is Biblical Israel?'

'Well, there is a minimalist position. To Wadi El Arish in the South.' That was in Egypt. 'To the Litani in the North.' That was in Lebanon. 'In the East, the Western part of Jordan, where the desert begins.'

So that meant seizing chunks of three neighbouring countries, and that was the minimalist position. What was maximalist? The response to this question was vaguer, but Kahane did mention the possibility of including in Israel the southern part of Syria, 'to where the Tigris and Euphrates meet'.

The Bible seemed quite an expansionist travel guide, particularly since I recalled that the Euphrates flowed through northern Syria and the Tigris did not flow through Syria at all, only through Iraq.

Kahane could see that I was making these mental notes, and he set out to put me right: 'We won't start a war to get it. But it we are attacked, the territory conquered shall be retained.'

He digressed to talk about his fellow-Israelis, whom he so despised. 'They are hobby Jews,' he said.

Then, at random, with no necessary logical connection, Kahane made this series of statements: 'What will be will not be what we want, but what God wants.' 'Judaism is truth. People cannot have the right to choose falsehood.' 'There will be democracy for all Jews provided that they don't break Jewish law.' 'Every Arab in this country is a good Arab, that is, an Arab who does not want to live in a Jewish state.' 'The Arab wants to live in a desert.' 'The *Sabra* – the Israeli-born Jew – does not know who he is since he does not know anti-Semitism or Judaism.' 'I understand Arabs. They understand me.' 'The obvious answer is to complete the exchange of population that began in 1948.' 'In Judaism there is no such concept as a non-Jewish citizen of a Jewish state.' 'A non-Jew in Israel can have personal rights but not national rights.'

I asked: 'So Arabs in Israel would be made unwelcome by being deprived by you of rights of citizenship. You want them to leave. But would they leave?'

He replied, seriously: 'They would leave because they fear Kahane. If they didn't go, we'd throw them out. We'd offer compensation. Compensation to those who leave quickly and quietly.'

I really wanted to get to the root of his thought. I asked: 'But this is their country, where they have their homes and jobs. What if they did not go quickly and quietly?'

'Most would go. A large number would not.'

I pressed him: 'So how would you get rid of those who did not go?'

'Force would certainly have to be used on them.'

I pursued his argument closely, to prevent him dodging: 'Would force include killing?'

He said, almost matter-of-factly: 'We would kill them if necessary.'

Here it was then, the final option listed in Rabbi Hess's article 'The Commandment of Genocide in the Torah'. Kahane added, coldly: 'I am not about to lose my state to bullets or to babies.'

There was nothing more that needed to be said. I made a perfunctory farewell, went down the dark stairway and emerged into the sunlight and bustle of Machanei Yehuda. Here were nice Jews, joyful Jews, Jews one could joke with.

Yet here in Jerusalem lived Jews who had contributed to the 26,000 votes that had helped Kahane to be elected to the Knesset.

I took a look at the transcript of Kahane's interview with the BBC. It ended with this quotation from him: 'The overwhelming majority of Jews in this country think what I say. They haven't got the courage to say it.'

It was certainly true that Kahane's views were, in some ways, the cold-bloodedly logical extension of what Raful Eitan had said to me, were the most explicit statement of Judaic Khomeinism that I had ever heard.

Did many of the lively, life-loving people of Machanei Yehuda really agree with the vileness that Kahane had been spewing out to me? I though not. I hoped not. Yet after an hour enclosed with him in that spider's web of an office, the defiling effect of his words would take time to fade.

6

The Air Pocket

I was going to a party. Israelis are tremendously hospitable. They will invite you to anything, even the most intimate celebrations within their family, a moment after having met you for the first time. So when my friend Yehiel, chairman of the World Labour Zionist movement, asked his hosts if he could bring me along to their Chanukah party, they agreed without hesitation.

We arrived at a not very large apartment in a middle-class suburb of Jerusalem. The only way to get rich in Israel is by being a huge success in business (or through corruption, an avenue chosen by a disconcertingly large number of otherwise blameless and family-loving persons). Israelis in public service, and that includes members of the Knesset, are paid utterly miserable sums. The people I was going to meet tonight were some of the most influential in their country's old Establishment. They included senior figures (or retired senior figures) in the civil service, the Labour and trade union movement and the armed forces. The acknowledged star among them – clever, merry and scintillating – was Simcha Dinitz, whom I had first met when he was head of Golda Meir's prime ministerial office, who later became Ambassador to Washington, and who in the election a few months before at the age of fifty-five just squeaked in as a first-term Labour Knesset member.

We arrived and, as at any middle-class party, there was a flurry of cooing, kissing and removal of coats. The guests were seated in comfortable chairs around a low table. Israeli parties are not the kind where you stand around with a glass in your hand, partly because not many Israelis drink alcohol very much. Instead you sit down and, simultaneously, you start talking and you start eating. So that is what happened on this occasion when I arrived with my fried Yehiel and his wife. There was one change in behaviour brought about by my arrival. All of these people, who had naturally been talking in their own language, Hebrew, immediately switched to speaking English, to each other as well as to me, so that I should not feel left out. Israelis are not only extremely hospitable, they are also, despite their on some occasions justified reputation for being rough-and-ready in their manners, extraordinarily courteous to guests.

Now they talked about art, about music, and above all about politics. Their talk was funny and often entertainingly malicious. One of those present told a long story about how Ben-Gurion as Prime Minister had appointed a man called Philip Sasson as Minister of Police in one of his several governments. I am not sure if I have got all the details of this story right, since it was quite complicated. However, the nub of it was that this man Sasson misunderstood what he was being offered. He was at the time an Israeli Ambassador, in Switzerland, I think, and he got a message saying that Ben-Gurion wanted him to become a Minister instead; Israeli public life is flexible enough for people to be switched, if it is required, from a civil service job to a party political appointment.

Sasson was loyal, and agreed to accept the new job even though he regarded it as a demotion, Ambassador being higher up in the diplomatic scale than Minister at an embassy. It was then explained to him that he was to be a Minister in a government, and that this was higher than Ambassador, so that it was a promotion after all. In the course of this anecdote, the point was made that for some reason Prime Ministers always tried to appoint their Ministers of Police (such as Shlomo Hillel, now Speaker of the Knesset) from among the Sephardi population. 'Maybe', said the story-teller, 'it's because most of the criminals are Sephardis and so they like to feel they have one of their own as Police Minister.'

This, in its way, was quite a racialist joke, though certainly not meant in any nasty way. I looked around the room and decided, from what I could make of the dozen or so guests eating busily away at plates full of latkes, accompanied by an excellent savoury dip, and occasionally sipping at glasses of hot punch, that all of them were Ashkenazis and therefore unlikely to be annoyed by this remark.

It also occurred to me that, as Ashkenazis, ten years ago they would in their different ways have been running the country as part of the Labour Government. Now, after seven years of the Likud in power and even with a Labour Prime Minister in office again at the head of the National Unity Government, they had been shoved towards the margins of their country; still influential, disproportionately so, but no longer the unquestioned bosses. Here they were at this cosy party behaving as if nothing had changed. Yet I knew, from the statistics made available to me, however haphazardly, by Dr Shemer, and from what Dr Lissak had explained to me, that these people were increasingly becoming a besieged minority. Others, rougher and cruder, were taking over the country.

I turned to the man sitting next to me, a former extremely senior civil servant, and said of my fellow guests: 'Don't they realize that things have changed? How can they go on behaving as though nothing has happened when the whole country is in turmoil around them and they are losing the power they used to have?'

He replied: 'They are living in an air pocket.'

As I travelled around Israel in succeeding weeks, I saw that this was true. Social change was changing Israel: irrevocably, if half of what Drs Shemer and Lissak had told me was accurate. Yet the Ashkenazi establishment was bravely, foolhardily, sometimes blindly, carrying on as if the old ways could survive permanently.

I went to an amateur concert at Tel Aviv University. The audience were, presumably, mostly relatives of those who were to play in the orchestra. The conductor came forward but, instead of starting the music right away, introduced his players. This one was a bank clerk, that an engineer. This was a reserve officer, that a schoolboy. The conductor went on to announce his orchestra's origins. Some were *Sabras*, born in Israel. Others came from America, from Russia. Apart from one of Bulgarian origin, all, so far as I could tell, were Ashkenazis.

When the concert was over, the audience did not go away just like that. It stayed around and gossiped. I was introduced to the soloist, and congratulated her. She told me that she was in the army, and had accordingly found practising and rehearsing a bit difficult, since she was not always available when the orchestra was. This, I realized, was part of the difficulty of doing anything in beleaguered Israel. I also realized that I was in a beleaguered Israel within a beleaguered Israel.

Here at this concert at this university, I was watching Ashkenazis watching Ashkenazis. It was the Israel I had grown used to over a quarter of a century, the Israel I loved. It was, however, the old Israel, an Israel on the defensive, possibly a doomed Israel. I was in the air pocket.

As the days and weeks went by, I alternated between life in this air pocket and the real Israel that was growing and changing outside it. Within the air pocket, life was much cosier.

In Gordon Street (Tel Aviv) were to be found galleries stocking the whole spectrum of modern art – from massively expensive representational paintings to twisted pieces of metal and aircraft engines – as it had developed internationally in the Western world, the Ashkenazi world. All the gallery-owners I saw seemed to be Ashkenazis. I went to Francesco Rosi's film of *Carmen*, starring Placido Domingo, in a cinema in a converted building which used to belong to Histadrut, Israel's trade union federation, itself a bastion of Ashkenazi power for many years. The small audience in the freezing cinema all seemed to be Ashkenazi. I went to look at the excavations of the Cardo, Jerusalem's Oxford Street in Byzantine times. On the surface, where mobs struggled along narrow streets to look at this freshly revealed slice of Jerusalem, were a group of elegant and expensive shops – Mira's

Gallery, Sheba's Gifts, Jacqueline Gal's Boutique, Scharf's Furs – all, it seemed, owned by Ashkenazis.

I went again to Tel Aviv University, this time to Beit Hatefutzot, the remarkable Museum of the Diaspora. There was an exhibition about British Jewry which had been recommended to me, and which I decided to go and see. It was excellent; beautifully mounted, erudite, informative, attractive, and very moving. I was especially touched by the old photographs from Leeds, where I was born and grew up, and particularly by pictures of Joseph Porton's shop in North Street, with Joseph Porton himself standing outside it. I had known Mr Porton when I was a child, since my father had taken me to this establishment to buy simple Hebrew books. I inspected the other people, not many of them, who were also walking round this exhibition. I saw that it was an exhibition about Ashkenazis, mounted by Ashkenazis, and visited by Ashkenazis.

In Tel Aviv I went to another concert, this time a highly professional one. It was given by the Israel Philharmonic Orchestra, at the time in its 49th year. The audience, I could see right away, was as usual overwhelmingly Ashkenazi, very like that to be found in the Festival Hall in London; this was hardly surprising, since a large segment of Festival Hall concert patrons also consists of poeple who had been Jewish refugees from Germany and Austria.

The main works in the programme consisted of Beethoven's Emperor Concerto and Shostakovich's Fifth Symphony. There was also a brief, modern, Israeli work which I pounced upon like a beagle pursuing the scent. It was called Rondo on a Sephardic Theme. Was there, I wondered, a breach in the air pocket?

I read the programme note. The name of the composer was Oedoen Partos, it said, and went on to explain: 'When Partos settled in this country in 1938, he immediately became fascinated with the wealth of Near-Eastern Jewish folklore. Even when Partos adopted a much more contemporary musical idiom (after 1960), the Sephardic melos remained discernible in his works, at times prominently and overtly, at other times in covert hints.'

This was most interesting; this could be a breakthrough. However, when I made inquiries about Partos, I found that he had come to Israel not from Morocco or Iran but from Hungary. He was an Ashkenazi, who was examining and exploring the exotica of the Sephardi world from within the securities and certainties of the air pocket.

Benny had refused to come to the concert. He said he was ready to sit through boring meetings for me, but not through boring music. So when I next saw him I thrust into his hand the concert programme (with information supplied in both Hebrew and English). I had folded it open at the list of members of the orchestra.

'Go through those names', I commanded, 'and tell me how many of them are Sephardis.'

Benny stalled. He said that it was impossible to be sure, since some people who were immigrants would have Hebraicized their names, thus disguising their origin.

'Do your best,' I insisted. 'I'm not looking for mathematical exactitude. I just want a rough idea.'

So, grumbling but conscientious, he plodded his way through the tiny print in which some one hundred and twenty orchestral players were listed. He paused and pondered from time to time. Eventually he said: 'I think I am sure of these.' He pointed to a Shulamit Alkalay among the second violins and an Amihud Elroy among the violas.

'No more Sephardis?' I asked.

'No more that I am sure of,' he said irritably.

So, in this orchestra, one of the foremost orchestras in the world and one of Israel's greatest sources of pride, fewer than two per cent were Sephardis without doubt.

Another day I thought I would give Jews of every description a rest, and went to Ein Kerem, the small and almost ludicrously picturesque village outside Jerusalem which was the birthplace of John the Baptist. Just in front of the handsome but very gloomy church, I saw a shop selling tiles, and decided to go in and have a look. They were very nice tiles, and the person making them was a woman whose name, I now saw from the shop sign, was Sandra Aronson. Here in this lopsided little village – so cut off from busy life, despite its proximity to Jerusalem, that the Post Office could not even provide change and left me its creditor by several shekels – was another little branch of the air pocket.

When I got back to Jerusalem, Yehiel's office had called with great news. Yehiel had arranged for me to attend, the following day, an Assembly of the Young Leadership of the Labour Party. The Prime Minister, Shimon Peres himself, would be present.

The Assembly was to be held in the guest house of Ramat Rachel Kibbutz. Ramat Rachel, before the Six-Day War, used to be right on the frontier with Jordan and quite dangerous to visit. Now it was perfectly safe.

We drove there, and as we approached Ramat Rachel it was clear that this was to be quite a major happening. On a piece of waste land outside the kibbutz entrance, a great many cars had already parked.

I walked along the path to the guest house, amid throngs of noisy, talkative people. At the entrance, there were one or two rather slovenly men in khaki uniforms who, so far as I could gather, were there to enforce security. If this was the best they could do for a meeting attended by the Prime Minister, I thought, then nobody in the country was safe; unless, of course, there was some cunning plan known only to Mossad or Shin Bet.

I fought my way up a narrow flight of stairs and came to a large room, crowded to bursting point. There were, as expected and indeed required, many young people, far more men than women. They were all drinking tea or coffee and eating cake.

There was a huge amount of enthusiastic greeting going on, and it was all very tactile. There was lots of embracing and punching among the men, all of whom seemed terrifically pleased to see each other.

Almost all the seats were now taken, and I was put at the end of a rear row. This position suited me fine, and I looked around. It was all very informal. There was hardly a tie to be seen in the place. Standard dress seemed to be sweaters and corduroy trousers; there was little denim being worn. I counted carefully, and could only see a couple of skullcaps. The Labour Party was confirming its reputation as a secular organization. I cast my gaze carefully around, but could not see a single man wearing an ear-ring, and there was quite certainly no-one present with hair dyed blue or green, or styled into a coxcomb.

The room was pretty crowded by now, with spectators standing along the walls on both sides. Greetings continued, and I was introduced to a great many people, all of whom, without exception, invited me to visit their homes or villages, in various parts of the country.

The meeting had been due to start at 6 p.m. but no-one took much notice of that. Indeed, it came as a distinct surprise when the Prime Minister arrived as early as 6.20. Here he came, accompanied by his personal bodyguards, two very dangerous-looking young men, and a bespectacled functionary whom I later discovered to be his press secretary.

Peres was neatly dressed in a suit and tie. He was presented by two small children with a huge bouquet which was quite difficult for them to carry. Peres accepted this with a smile, and then sat down beneath a banner of red, white and blue. He instantly started to smoke. He was brought a glass of orange juice, and drank that right off.

The chairman began the proceedings, and in the course of his opening remarks announced my presence. This aroused considerable applause, somewhat to my surprise, since I doubted whether many in this gathering had ever heard of me.

While this fellow was droning on, I heard a conversation between two men behind me, discussing the size of the audience, now several hundred strong: 'Where did they all come from?' 'The question is, who paid them to come?'

The chairman announced that first there would be some opening speeches, and then there would be questions, and finally the Prime Minister would respond. I listened very carefully, but it was impossible for me to tell when the speeches left off and the questions began, since all contributions seemed about the same length, and many of them were expostulations.

I was unable to understand why some speakers were popular and others not. Audience reaction did not appear to depend on what they said. For example, a thickset man with a moustache was very well applauded. On the other hand, a little, handsome man in black with a mop of black hair did not receive a single clap. Both talked about the Lebanon war and apparently were in agreement about it – that is, against it. The third speaker, a neat, bespectacled man in a jacket with a sweater underneath, got no hearing at all, his remarks being drowned by a hum of conversation. Throughout, the Prime Minister smoked and looked interested. The room was geting hotter, and more orange juice was sent for.

A thin, drooping man, wearing a jacket, open-necked shirt and slacks, addressed himself directly to Peres, possibly asking an actual question. He got into a muddle but it did not matter, since there was now a continual buzz of talk.

Then, after all these quite run-of-the-mill people, came an Arab. He shook the Prime Minister's hand, and the conversations stopped (after some hushings). He was very thin, and wore a proper two-piece suit, the general effect of stylishness being a little impaired because he did not have a tie on. He spoke in Hebrew, attacked Rabbi Kahane, seemed the best orator so far, and was well applauded.

Next came a woman, so tiny that her face did not show above the top of the rostrum. This aroused laughter, but she did not mind. She wore a pale pink cotton blouse and a grey skirt. She was pert and self-confident. She spoke loudly and hectored Peres. 'We want to withdraw from Lebanon immediately,' she shouted. 'We want to hear it from you short and sharp.' This caused a wave of amusement, but she still did not care. She had had her say.

After her the next speaker was a big, burly man in a polo-necked sweater. He came from Haifa. His hair was tinged with grey, even though he was part of the young leadership of the party.

Altogether there were fourteen of these people. Two were particularly popular. One was a little, stout, stocky, untidy, blond, bearded man. He had his hands in his pockets and his sleeves were rolled up. He spoke in an irritated, complaining tone, getting louder as he went on. He was clapped enthusiastically. The other was a fat woman called Dalia, who caused a sensation when she announced that the government hadn't got balls. Of the thirteen Jews, at most four were Sephardis, and they were the only ones who spoke about the problems of the Sephardis, which were the problems of the poor and neglected. Most of the rest were preoccupied with the Lebanon War which, in the way they discussed it, was proprietorially an Ashkenazi issue.

These speeches went on and on, and I did admire Shimon Peres for the way he sat though them all, very patiently, apparently listening with care, smoking all the time.

He was not called upon to speak until 7.33 p.m. He started with some jokes. He was good, no doubt about it, very professional, very polished; but his style did not go down well with this audience. He tried to explain to them the problems of being the head of a government he had been unable to choose, and the need for him to behave in a manner acceptable to the religious groups whose support Labour needed. So far as I could tell, he was the only speaker, apart from the Sephardis, who spoke about the problem of the ethnic split in Israel, and how it had widened during the seven years of Likud government.

Peres spoke for an hour. He often failed to hold his audience. They were, understandably, preoccupied with the Lebanon War. Yet they did not seem to regard this conflict as a symptom of something more profoundly worrying that was happening in their country. They believed, so far as I could tell, that if only Israel withdrew, the problem was solved. They did not appear to understand that the invasion was the result of processes within their country which would continue to cause upheavals long after Israeli troops finally left Lebanon. They looked at the Lebanon problem with Ashkenazi eyes, and did not seem to realize that the problems of the Sephardis, unless faced, could prevent a majority Labour government from winning office – and only Labour could put an end to outbreaks of military adventurism.

After some two and a half hours, the meeting ended. We

wandered out into the night, down the path, out of the kibbutz gates, and towards our car. It was winter in Jerusalem, the stars shining fiercely away in a black sky. Jerusalem is cold in winter, and the night was very chilly indeed. As we walked, we were passed by an old man. He was naked except for a pair of flimsy white shorts. He was jogging. He was oblivious to us as we walked by. He was in his own private world, his own air pocket. And although he was all by himself, he was little more isolated from what was really happening to his country than the crowds of charming, idealistic, good-natured, enthusiastic, noisy Ashkenazi socialists who in little groups went their ways into the Jerusalem darkness.

7

Three Villages

These were beautiful days. I had visited Israel on many occasions, summer and winter; but it was a long time since I had driven around so many different bits of it, and this was such a kind winter, so mild, so comfortable for touring and seeing places I had seen before and other places I was visiting for the first time. I thought I was used to Israel, accustomed to all it could hold for me, even a bit irritated with its over-familiarity. Yet I was finding myself falling in love with this land all over again.

Today I was driving out of Israel itself, into the West Bank. Yehiel had fixed up for me to go to one of the notorious West Bank settlements and, on the way back, to visit a newish kibbutz in the Jordan valley.

So out of Jerusalem we rode again, but this time roughly northwards. As we left the limits of the city, Benny said to me: 'You don't need to wear your seat belt now if you don't want to. Israeli law doesn't apply here.' Virtuously, I went on wearing it.

We went through the Arab towns of Al-Bireh and Ramallah. They were ugly places, made up of square, blunt boxes of buildings, some constructed of stone, some faced with stone.

Then we were out into the countryside. Occasional knots of Israeli soldiers were to be seen, reminding me that we were in occupied territory, a place that had been under foreign rule for nearly twenty years now. We passed a huge training base, bristling with artillery and tanks. We passed a Jewish settlement, Beit El, the House of the Lord, and here too the houses looked like boxes.

The odd donkey trundled along. A jeep rolled by, crammed with sheep. We were among hills now, wonderful brown, rolling hills covered in olive groves. It was here, Benny reminded me, that years ago we had watched a scene from *Jesus Christ Superstar* being filmed.

Now we passed Arab villages. They nestled fluently in the folds of the rock-strewn hills. Some of the houses were white, others blue. They looked as if a child had painted them on to the hillsides.

Above was a limpid, cloudless blue sky. We were being bathed in some of the loveliest light in the world, light that was soft but crisp. It showed us, as if outlined by the sharpest possible fine pencil point, stone terraces and minarets of distant mosques. On the roofs of the houses, television aerials stood out as if woven by spiders.

Yehiel had provided us with a guide, a young Canadian Jew called David. He came from Vancouver and was now a pioneer. David showed me a map of the West Bank. It looked as though it had been infected with an outbreak of measles. These measle spots were the Jewish settlements, and right away I was full of hostility against them. David pointed to a settlement on top of a hill we were passing. A road snaked upwards to the distant houses. 'That road is no more than two months old,' David told me.

On the other side of the main road, an Arab was milking a cow in a field. Another Arab in another field was following a horse with a wooden plough.

David explained everything to me. He was very nice and very young and, like many educated young men and women from the other side of the Atlantic, he employed jargon as if it was a language of its own.

A road sign had on it: 'Tomb of Joshua Son of Nun', with an arrow. How was it possible to cope with a country which had notices like that? No normal criteria were suitable or appropriate. In this unbelievable countryside, an Arab lazily drove a herd of ambling goats and behind him the red hills faded away to the horizon. On top of a hill on

75

the other side of the road, an Arab village was smeared like white icing.

A dead donkey lay by the side of the military road that cut through this occupied land. Then, on yet another hillside, a Jewish settlement sat untidily like an excrescence. It was impossible to believe that those who had designed and fashioned these glaring red roofs had any feeling for the land.

I mentioned my sentiments to David, and he told me that he shared them. 'What can we do to combat that phenomenon?' he asked plaintively.

Another village, an Arab village, sat on a hilltop as if growing out of it. Another Jewish settlement sprouted tower blocks. Then, at last, we were arriving in an area colonized by Gush Emunim, the Block of the Believers. In this region of Samaria, about fifty miles north of Jerusalem, forty miles north-east of Tel Aviv, was situated the settlement we were visiting, Kedumim, a further litter of red-roofed villas thrown at random on to a hillside. We turned off the road, drove up the hill, passed a bank (owned by a religious group) and some nondescript buildings, and arrived in the town centre.

I already had some idea of what kind of opinions I was likely to encounter in this place from studying its returns in the previous July's Knesset election. Raful's Tehiya party had emerged top with 145 votes. Next came Morasha, an extreme orthodox religious faction, with 115. Likud had won 43 votes, Kahane's Kach party 10. Labour had come bottom of the poll, with the support of precisely two inhabitants of Kedumim.

David, who had been here before, led us to a sizeable hut. There, waiting eagerly, perhaps predatorily, was Rachel. She was a nicely dressed woman, sharp-featured, bespectacled, middle-aged. She sat down with us at a table. I was going to have to put up with the indoor briefing that I knew awaited me. It was, indeed, part of what I had come for; but I longed to be out in the balmy open air, looking around instead of being talked at.

'This', said Rachel portentously, 'is the Academy of the Land of Israel.' She went on: 'Here in Israel not all the people understand the importance of Jews settling in Israel.'

I had known I was going to be hostile, but I had not known that I would become hostile so quickly. 'Why do you call this Israel?' I asked, deliberately provocative. 'This is not the state of Israel.'

Rachel, who was clearly used to people like me and worse than me, said comfortably, in no way perturbed: 'We have it according to the Bible.' I was going to get a dose of Maimonides interpreted by Nachmanides.

I realized, looking at Rachel, watching her failing in any way to be provoked by me, that she was the Jewish equivalent of a Born-Again Christian. Her certainties were not going to be troubled by my irreverent irrelevancies. Her attitude stimulated me to be, if anything, even more ill-behaved.

'This is territory occupied by your army,' I asserted accusingly.

She had her answer ready: 'We are not conquerors. We are ready to live with these people as neighbours. But they do not accept us. It is not our problem. It is their problem.'

She kept on saying maddening things, meaningless things: 'Israel are the people of the Bible.' 'This land and especially this area was given to us by God.'

She was intense. She smiled constantly. She would not stop to allow discussion. Even to ask questions I had to interrupt, quite rudely. I realized that my rudeness did not matter, was not even noticed by her. It was impossible to communicate with her. She did not really hear what I had to say.

Instant coffee and sweet biscuits were brought in. We continued, I trying to break down her complacency, she absolutely impervious to my attempts.

'You conquered this territory,' I said threateningly.

'We did not conquer it,' she replied calmly. 'We took it back.'

'How could you take it back when it was not yours? It is not inside the borders of Israel; I do not have to wear my seat-belt when I am here.'

'This', she said, 'is a big mistake.'

I was not clear whether she meant that my not having to wear a seat-belt was a big mistake or, more largely, the failure to incorporate the West Bank into Israel. Whatever it was she meant, she had no doubt what had to be done: 'This is a big mistake,' she repeated. 'We are trying to change it. This is our land.'

Now we were joined by a small, compact man, quite young, dressed in a dark suit and wearing a beard. This was Rabbi Atlas, and he was a big noise among the settlers. In an American accent he immediately began to tell me about all the things that Israel had done to help the Arabs in this territory.

'You mean on the West Bank?' I asked.

'I do not accept you calling it the West Bank,' said Rachel. 'This is Judea and Samaria.'

Benny, who had, for him, been remarkably silent, now wickedly asked Rachel: 'Why do you only claim the West Bank? The East Bank is mentioned in the Bible as well. Why don't you claim that?'

Rabbi Atlas replied for her: 'Because she is a moderate.'

Rachel, possibly because she was a moderate, more likely because she had served her purpose in saying her party piece as an exponent of the settlers' doctrine, was now dismissed. Rabbi Atlas took charge and led us out of the hut and down a path. We were in the soft fresh air again, but I was not to be permitted to enjoy it. I was, instead, to be subjected to an audio-visual display manufactured, so David confided in me, by the people responsible for the Israel Experience.

We entered another hut, the blinds were drawn, and the entertainment commenced. I noted right away that the production values were lavish, complete with stereophonic sound. A relentless commentary told how long ago the Jews who had wanted to come back to the land of Israel were offered Uganda instead. Then we were shown some of the holy sites in the West Bank, and the commentator declared: 'Without these places the state of Israel would be the equivalent of a Jewish land in Uganda.'

The film displayed pictures of places in the West Bank where Jews used to live before the Arabs took over, places from which Jews had been evicted by Arabs. Viewers were invited to regard this eviction as an outrage, and I had no difficulty in doing so. At the same time, I wondered if those who made the film, and those like Rabbi Atlas who showed it as propaganda from their argument, realized that the case they were making was identical with that of the Palestine Liberation Organization. The Palestinians similarly, in their material, made a point of showing pictures of houses in Haifa and Jaffa from which Arabs had been displaced by Jews. Did they realize that the Palestinians had their own propaganda which was the mirror image of the Jew's Zionist propaganda, using the same arguments in reverse, evoking identical emotions?

The film ground on, filled with happy, smiling Jews who had returned to their heritage. 'We have fulfilled a verse from the scriptures,' rejoiced the hearty commentator, as on the wide screen faces of Jews multiplied and multiplied again, until there were dozens and dozens of settlers rejoicing at their return to this particular portion of the land of the Bible. The audio-visual presentation ended. The blinds were raised.

Rabbi Atlas looked to me for a reaction. 'It's really an argument for *Lebensraum*, isn't it?' I asked, nastily.

The rabbi said, firmly: 'If we do not settle Judea and Samaria, millions of Arabs will migrate here and establish an Arab majority in the land of Israel.'

He was advancing the case set out in Professor Tal's disturbing lecture.

I was appalled. 'That is a really racialist argument,' I said.

The rabbi was impervious. 'We are still only the bridgehead,' he insisted. He kept on making comments, with the utmost conviction and satisfaction, that each raised a point that would have taken half an hour to dispute. This, of course, is the technique of the skilled controversialist, and Rabbi Atlas was both highly skilled and extremely controversial.

'As a Jew and therefore a Zionist,' he began one sentence, categorically, though of course it is perfectly possible to be a Jew without being a Zionist.

When I asked him why he had come to Israel from America, he responded: 'I returned home.' How could he return to a place where he had never been before, I wondered. I knew I would never get an answer to that question, even if I got an opportunity to put it, which was doubtful, since the rabbi never seemed to stop talking. Settlement in the land of Israel was not an *option*, he continued: 'We accept our obligation.'

When I did manage to squeeze a word into his relentless monologue, he never met my argument. He simply slid round it. 'We need co-existence,' he announced; but then he continued: 'We are dealing with a people whose mentality is such that they can love you like a brother one day and hate you as an enemy for the next thousand years.'

He argued like an Arab bigot or like any other obsessive. I decided that if I had to put up with any more of this, I wanted to do so in the open air. I said I would like a stroll around this settlement, and he courteously agreed.

We went out of the hut, into the clean light of day. A hawk hovered in the sky. We walked along a little uphill path, past a small shop where a couple of people were chatting at the door. I suddenly realized that, apart from Rabbi Atlas and the ineffable Rachel, these were the only people I had seen in Kedumim. Where was everybody?

There were the houses they presumably lived in, compact little prefabs with little gardens. Some of the houses were dripping with foliage. Along the paths, ripe pomegranates hung from the trees. I looked around me, at lemon trees and rose trees. It was very nice. Rabbi Atlas droned on. 'Violence is part and parcel of the Arab culture,' he insisted. 'This is against the Judaeo-Christian ethic.'

He pointed out to me in the distance a neighbouring Arab village, called Kafr Kadum, and I asked how the people of his settlement got on with their neighbours.

Rabbi Atlas dodged the question. 'We need co-existence,' he said.

'What do you mean by co-existence?' I asked. 'On a national or personal level?'

'We can't live on a personal level,' he replied. 'Neither side wants to have social relations or inter-marriage.'

He then went on to larger topics. 'It is impossible for Arabs to accept a peace agreement,' he said.

'Then how do you explain what Sadat did with Begin?'

'Sadat was using peace as a tactic. He didn't really want it.'

We strolled along in the soft sunshine. We were now on a paved road, lined with villas which were really rather big. A large blue plastic slide decorated a children's sandpit, though no children were playing in it.

I was baffled by what Sadat had been up to with his tactic of pretending to want peace, and asked for a further explanation.

'The Arabs don't believe in making peace,' Atlas repeated.

'But what about Egypt?'

'No-one can believe that the peace agreement with Egypt will hold. The Arabs have a culture that believes in war as a concept.'

Benny and David, who understandably had had enough of all this, had peeled off to get the car. Now they drove up and I got in. Rabbi Atlas was still talking. I thanked him for his time and we drove down the hill from Kedumim.

I was in a rage. I had expected to be annoyed. I had not anticipated anything as bad as this. 'I want to drive into the next Arab village and talk to the people there,' I said to David. 'I must find out what they think.'

So we drove on, and soon saw an Arab village on a slope by the side of the road. We turned off, and stopped at a shop. An elderly Arab came to the door and Benny, displaying a knowledge of spoken Arabic that much impressed David, asked where we could find the *mukhtar*. The man pointed uphill.

This village was called Berka. The narrow streets were unpaved. Streams of water ran down the middle of these paths, apparently the only form of drainage that existed. Tiny children with huge brown eyes played in litter-strewn open patches. Women walked along balancing plastic containers on their heads. Donkeys carried more plastic containers. Cactuses grew by the side of the paths.

We drove through this sleepy, dirty little place looking for the *mukhtar* or anyone else who could speak to me in English. We came to large blue gates, but no-one answered to our knocking. Women directed us, but their directions seemed to lead nowhere. A youth paused by a gate, and

Benny interrogated him. All he would say was, 'Our neighbours here is very good people.' This was scarcely enough. We turned, and the youth followed us as we went back the way we had come, past a cow tethered to a dead tree.

We came to a house, more of a shanty, really, made of rough concrete. We peeped through the gate, and saw several women at a kind of outdoor stove, and tiny children at a small table eating what appeared to be a very appetising meal. A little man with a moustache came out, holding worry-beads in his hand. Benny asked in Arabic if he spoke English, and the man said yes. I said that I would welcome talking to him if he was willing, and he replied that he was.

He popped back through the gate, and emerged carrying stools. We sat down, the four of us, in the sunlight and surrounded by the smell of shit.

This man was called Mahmoud Haj Mohammed. I asked him if the Haj in his name meant that he had made the pilgrimage to Mecca and he said yes, he had gone there in 1977. He wore a shirt with a sweater over it, canvas trousers and sandals, and had a skullcap on his head. I asked him his age and he said he was sixty. He looked much older.

He was proud of his English, which he had learned during seven years' service in the Palestine Police. I tried to find out what he thought about the Jews who lived nearby, and how he felt about being ruled by Israelis. I had to coax the answers out of him. That this should be so was hardly surprising. After all, he had no reason to trust me and no real idea of what I was up to.

'We have no troubles with the Jews,' he said. 'There are no accidents between us and them. If there is no cheating, we can live happily with the Jews.'

I asked him how Israeli occupation compared with life when the West Bank had been part of Jordan.

'The Jews are better than Hussein,' he asserted. This did not, however, mean that they were perfect. 'When we go to complain to the police, they hear from the people over there and they do not hear from us. But we would like to live with them as brothers and friends.'

I asked if he would prefer Yasser Arafat to come and take

over from the Israelis.

'We do not know what Arafat is like,' Mahmoud Haj Mohammed replied cautiously.

A stout woman, in a long, voluminous, untidy dress, brought out glasses of tea on a decorated tray and handed them round. I asked where the water for the tea had come from.

This question impelled Mahmoud to be more indignant than he had been so far. 'Our village has no running water, no electricity,' he complained. 'We asked the Jews. They promise us. But the Jews do not help us.'

I sipped the tea. It had a pungent, ingratiating taste. Some kind of herb had been added to provide this flavour. A long, untidy line of small children, all with huge satchels on their backs, walked by, staring at us curiously.

I asked Mahmoud about health provision in the village. Once again he was annoyed. There was no ambulance for people who had to be taken to hospital, he said. The caution that had governed his earliest remarks had been forgotten in the flow of grievances. But now he had run out of things to say.

I thanked him for speaking to us so openly. He smiled, shook my hand. We got into our car and drove unsteadily down the rocky little road, out of Berka, as Mahmoud Haj Mohammed waved a somewhat uncertain goodbye. We went on our way, through the West Bank, past a Biblical sight of a flock of sheep being herded by a young shepherd.

David was most put out by what we had learned in Berka. 'It is a distortion of national priorities,' he said, a serious condemnation.

We came to Nablus, the largest city of the West Bank. Benny instructed me to look out for yellow Israeli car licence plates, as distinct from the light blue West Bank plates. He told me that I would see very few, and he was right. Not many Israelis drove into Nablus on casual visits, it seemed, whether from a lack of feelings of safety or simply a disinclination to be among people who did not want them there.

All the same, Nablus was very crowded. This was the

Biblical Shechem. There was food in amplitude, even super-fluity. Whatever the West Bank Arabs lacked in democratic freedoms or even public utilities, they certainly were far from starving. Here was a cart overflowing with cauliflowers, there another full of bananas. A little mobile stall, selling steamed sweetcorn, came into view. The aroma was seductive, and I would have liked to stop for some, but we were very late now.

My last sight of Nablus was of a group of identifiable Israelis, an armed military patrol. As the road rose towards the entrance to the Judean desert, our path was blocked by a vast mob of goats, out of the control of their shouting goatherd. We edged our way through and then, on a pinnacle, came to what seemed to be a rough collection of stones placed in a circle. This, said Benny, was the remains of a Roman watchtower. The West Bank had had many occupants before the Israelis.

Down we drove, into the valley, past fields in which toma-toes grew and others in which turkeys strutted. We arrived in the kibbutz of Gilgal, a communal settlement established in 1973 by one of the kibbutz movements linked to the Labour Party. It was in the middle of the Judean Desert, only five miles west of the river Jordan, only five miles inside Israel.

We entered through the open, quite formidable gate. Gilgal looked a bit down-at-heel, and I was rather fed up that we were here at all. We had started out early. It had been a heavy day. Did I really want to spend time arguing ideology with a collection of humourless kibbutzniks?

David went into the makeshift little dining hall. A girl appeared, and told him firmly that the kitchen was closed. He began to argue. I left them to it, and walked into the sunlight, down here in the valley nicely warm, and looked around. There was some kind of sports ground, pretty bed-raggled. There was a meeting hall. On both sides were high, purple hills. I lay down on the springy lawn which formed a kind of village green for this little settlement. I dozed.

David came and fetched me. Food was ready in the dining hall. We sat at a table at one end, while at the other people swabbed down the floor. There was a lot to eat despite the kitchen having been closed. The most substantial dish was a fish and potato stew. This was rather cold, but that was nothing new on a kibbutz, where at the best of times the temperature of the food can be speculative. There were dishes of carrots, spinach, avocado pear – almost a weed in this part of the world – and tomatoes. There was also a strange little green fruit, very sweet and aromatic, that I had never seen before and whose English name no-one was able to tell me.

David asked if I would like to see a video-film about Gilgal. At the risk of disappointing him, I said that I would prefer to sit out on the lawn and talk to people. He went to fetch some conversationalists who could speak to me in English, and returned with two. One was the girl who had attempted to starve us, somewhat plump, who, as we greeted each other, produced the most beautiful smile I had seen for a long time, a smile that kept appearing as we talked. She had pleasant features and soft brown hair, and wore a cotton sweater, jeans and boots.

There was also a man, small and bespectacled, wearing a dark blue shirt and jeans. I asked them their names and ages. She was Tali. She was twenty-two years old, and had come from Tel Aviv. His name was Ishai. He was aged thirty-one. I did not find out where he came from. I questioned them, starting with Tali. I asked her why she was here, miles from anywhere, in this vulnerable and isolated area.

It was, she acknowledged, quite small. Just a hundred people lived here, thirty-two of them children. And it certainly was very difficult for young people to stay here.

'But', said Tali, smiling, 'when I came here on youth duty I fell in love with the place.'

I asked her what exactly she was doing here. This was not an urban settlement like Kedumim, right in the middle of an Arab population. Gilgal, like other kibbutzim in the Jordan Valley, had been established as part of the Allon Plan, worked out by one of Israel's legendary heroes, the late Yigal Allon. Allon had hoped that it would be possible for Israel to negotiate with Jordan a withdrawal from the heavily populated parts of the West Bank, while retaining a defensive line just west of the Jordan River. The negotiations, sadly, had never come about, but some of the settlements on the defensive line had been planted.

Tali said: 'We are making facts for the negotiations later. We believe that it helps to achieve a settlement.'

I told her and Ishai that the settlers at Kedumim had tried to persuade me that they had some mystical link with the land. Did they feel the same thing?

Tali replied: 'We are linked to the land because we are working it.'

I could have kissed her. I had spent most of the day getting increasingly angrier and more hostile to the Jews on the West Bank, and indeed quite hostile to the Jews in Israel generally. This unsophisticated girl, with one simple sentence, had revived my awareness of the genuine and selfless pioneering which existed among so many Israelis, but which was obscured by the sophistries of those smug opportunists who sought to ride on the backs of these true pioneers.

At the same time, as we sat in the soothing sun on this central lawn, I suddenly recollected that during my time in Kedumim I had seen hardly any people, apart from Rabbi Atlas and his acolyte Rachel, and had certainly not noticed anyone at work. Now I interrupted our conversation to ask Benny what the people of Kedumim and similar places did for a living.

'A lot of them go into the cities and work during the day, and they come home in the evenings.'

'You mean they are commuters!' I cried, suddenly seeing it all. 'They are commuter pioneers!'

I turned back to Tali. 'It is clear that you love this place,' I said. 'Would you be ready to give it up in return for peace?'

She replied: 'We have to build the trust. Then if the Arabs need this land, we will go, because peace is more important than anything.'

Ishai had been listening carefully, and now he interrupted. 'The Jordan Valley is a red line,' he said, fiercely. 'We can't do without it. If peace without the Jordan Valley or no peace with it, I choose no peace.'

So there we had the difference. The woman who would give up anything for peace, the man who insisted on retaining the minimal defensive line. Ishai now went away, to prepare tea in his house. Tali asked me if I would like to come and look at the date groves where she worked.

We strolled along, birds twittering overhead. Gilgal was, it appeared from what Tali told me, a luscious storehouse of tropical fruits. Here in this hot desert climate they grew grapes, lemons, bananas, mangoes. They had two crops of water melons every year. They cultivated cotton and bred turkeys.

I asked her if she did not feel vulnerable, so far from cities. 'I feel much safer than in Tel Aviv,' she replied.

We walked round the date groves. There were lots and lots of them. To me they were just trees, even if of a particularly exotic kind. To Tali they were her life. She told me about the harvesting of the dates. It sounded very hard work, but clearly she loved it.

We walked back up the hill, and along a little winding path betwen tiny houses, very different from the grand villas in the best part of Kedumim. In one of these small buildings was the couple of cramped rooms that constituted Ishai's home. We entered, and I was beckoned to sit down on a sofa. Next to my right shoulder was a bookshelf. Most of the books were in Hebrew. I did notice one in English, *Washington Square* by Henry James, a strange, precious work of fiction to be found in this wild place.

We were served tea and ginger cake, and we discussed the rights of Arabs under Israeli occupation. Tali was unsympathetic to provocative Jewish settlements among large Arab populations. To her the issue was quite clear.

'If there were Arab villages here, *we* wouldn't be here,' she said flatly, and flashed her lovely smile.

Ishai, though not quite such a dove as Tali on military matters, equalled her fervour about the need for Arab emancipation. 'We can't be democrats and hold a million Arabs without civil rights,' he insisted, and offered me some more cake.

It was time to go if we were to get to Jerusalem before

the early winter nightfall. We drove a little way south before turning west. We passed more flocks of goats, went by two Arab young men holding hands, arrived at a refugee camp, a mini-town of shanty blocks. This, said David, was where the film director Costa-Gavras had shot some of the scenes from his picture *Hannah K*, the story of a Jewish woman lawyer who defends a Palestinian on trial on terrorist charges.

We approached the outskirts of Jericho, a huge oasis in this wilderness, a green blot on the horizon which turned into a town. Stalls overflowed with the fruit produced here. Banana plantations flashed by. David kept us entertained with remarks delivered in his own special language: 'That's a very Western value judgement, I think . . . Your stimulation level is low.'

We climbed up the mountains, driving carefully along the perilously narrow roads that clung to the sides of precipices. Benny and I had driven once before along here, in the opposite direction, listening to news bulletins about the Israeli hostages being held by terrorists at the 1972 Olympic Games. The tension of this drive today was accompanied by the remembered tension at that time.

At a cliff edge there was a patch jutting out over the valley where drivers could park and gaze at the yellow moonscape that was the astonishing view from here. Stationed on this precarious vantage-point was a car, and standing beside it three people. One of them was Rachel from Kedumim, showing the land of her heritage to a couple of tourists who looked as though they were somewhat more amenable and responsive than I. She saw us, she recognized us, but not a flicker of acknowledgement crossed her face. We were failures to be wiped from her memory.

A black cloud glowered from the sky. The sun was squarely behind it, so that the cloud's entire outline was rimmed in gold. The sight was beautiful, but at the same time somehow terrifying. This tint of sunlight cast a strange yellow glow on the black tents of the Beduin that we passed.

Then, in the distance, Jerusalem came into view. We had driven that day in a loop that was almost a circle. In a few hours we had been in three different worlds. We had visited

Jews who were self-centred, narrow-minded and bigoted, who, if they cared at all about democracy, cared about it only for themselves. In Kedumim, rationality and democracy were on the defensive, standing with their backs to the wall. Nachmanides and Maimonides reigned supreme.

We had visited Arabs who, almost certainly, were at least as well off as they had ever been, possibly better off than they might have been had the Israelis never conquered their homes. Yet they saw, a few minutes away, other people being given huge sums of government money to enhance living standards incomparably better than they themselves could ever hope for. The contrast was degrading to those responsible for it, for those who justified it, for those who tolerated it even by acquiescence.

Then, as I was thinking black thoughts about what had become of the once idealistic state of Israel, we had arrived at the little settlement of Gilgal and found decent young people who might be muddled about what ought to be done, but whose moral instincts were a justification for all those who wanted to think well of Israel. The question I asked, as we drove up to the Sonesta Hotel for a shower and a meal, was, simply, how many Rabbi Atlases were there for each Ishai, how many Rachels for each Tali, how many hard glances of intolerance and bigotry for each lovely, loving smile?

8

Two Moroccans

It was far too early. I had got up not much after six in order to go to Sderot. I did not want to go to Sderot. I was not even sure why I was going to Sderot. My friend Yehiel had arranged it all for me, because he thought it would be interesting. I did not have the heart to tell him that I had been to lots of development towns in southern Israel, and that one more was sure to be like every other I had seen.

Buried away in my mind was the thought that I might back out of this trip at the last minute. I might change my mind and, instead of going south, veer north and go up to Acre, where Rabbi Kahane was due that day to make one of his disruptive forays into an Arab area.

We drove out of the hotel gates and through the Jerusalem suburbs. I had to admit that the city looked marvellous on this sunny winter morning: not just the ancient historic city with its creamy yellow walls giving the impression that they were made of crumbly gingerbread; but even the hideous tower blocks, even the ghastly Hilton, sticking up into the sky like a monstrous gangrenous finger. Almost everything seemed beautiful, bathed in a golden light and softened by a light mist.

We were not going straight to Sderot. That was another thing that annoyed me. First we were going to another development town called Beit Shemesh, where we were to pick up some man who had been mayor. I really did not know why we had to take this person with us. Benny was driving me, so I had company and, if I needed one, an interpreter;

but Yehiel had arranged it all, and Yehiel had taken so much trouble to help me that I had to comply. In addition, this man was waiting and there was no way of contacting him to put him off. As I rode along on this heart-rendingly lovely day, I began hardening my heart, ready to tell this unwanted passenger that we were going to Acre after all and that neither his company nor his services (unspecified) were required.

Beit Shemesh, though, was waiting for us. Two scruffy men, middle-aged, were standing on the pavement of what seemed to be the main thoroughfare. They could tell we were strangers immediately, because Benny is very blond, a colour of hair not often seen in development towns. They called out, in Hebrew, 'Amram Luk is waiting for you. Turn round.'

Obediently, we turned. There, on the other side of the road, was another middle-aged man, not scruffy, respectably if shabbily dressed in a brown suit with a little cardigan underneath because it was, after all, winter. He was dark, and burnished still darker by the sun. He had a small, greying moustache. The moment I saw him I realized that we could not possibly scrap our arrangements and go to Acre instead of Sderot. Sderot it would have to be. Amram Luk had clearly set aside his whole day to escort us, and it would be intolerable not to accept his benevolence.

We drove along in the benign sunshine, between groves filled with orange trees so richly laden that the fruit was too heavy to remain attached to the branches and was falling off, almost as we watched. Cypress trees lined the road. It was so nice that I even began to become reconciled to the idea of going to boring Sderot.

There Amram Luk sat in the little car, and I decided that I had better find out if there was anything interesting about him. He spoke English reasonably well, and I asked him question after question.

He told me that he was an immigrant from Morocco. He had come to Israel in 1956. The élite of Moroccan Jews, he said, had gone to France and made good there. The others had come to Israel. He was one of the others. His father had been a shopkeeper.

Amram Luk had been 24 years old when he came to Israel. He ended up in Beit Shemesh in the way that many Jews from North Africa and other poor areas had ended up in development towns. He had done well in Beit Shemesh.

He had become the mayor, a Labour mayor, even though Beit Shemesh did not vote Labour in Parliamentary elections. He had stayed mayor for twelve years, but finally the voters had thrown him out. Now he worked as a regional official of the Labour Party. He had been Number 72 on the Labour Party's list of candidates in the July general election. Labour had won only 44 seats and there was no way that it was ever going to get enough votes to win 72 out of the total of 120. Amram had been a make-weight, nothing more.

He had been used; but he was no fool. He was a faithful Labour supporter, knowing he had been used and despite having been used by Labour.

'Why,' I asked him, 'are you still Labour when they would not put you higher than 72 on the list?'

'Because it is the less bad,' said Amram Luk.

His work in Israel, his time in Beit Shemesh, he told me, were to him part of the pioneering period of Israel. He was very proud to have been a pioneer. But what had been pioneering to him, he said, was regarded by today's young Moroccans as an entrenchment of inferiority.

'The young Moroccans are less patient than their parents,' said Amram. 'To our young people, the Labour Party is the Establishment, the Histadrut is the Establishment, the kibbutzim are the Establishment, the Ashkenazis are the Establishment.'

As I listened to this wise and dignified man, I saw clearly why Yehiel had thought I should meet him. I still did not see why we had to meet on the road to Sderot. Still, as we drove along between the fruitful fields, to Sderot we were going and I went on questioning Amram Luk.

He told me of the conflicts in this part of Israel. On the one hand there were the development towns, inhabited by poor people, Sephardis, who had only their labour to sell. On the other hand there were the rich kibbutzim run by Ashkenazis, which had opened regional factories to centralize use of their output and at the same time, in response to urgings from David Ben-Gurion when he was Prime Minister, to provide employment for the Orientals living in these areas.

In one way the plan did work. The factories provided jobs, and the jobs were needed. But the kibbutzniks, the idealistic socialists, took on the role of capitalistic employers and, instead of being regarded as benefactors, were resented. So thousands of Oriental Jews, working in chicken-slaughtering plants, in dairies, in cotton gins, in fruit-packing factories and canning factories, felt that to the kibbutzniks, with their much better living conditions, they were just cheap labour.

Benny, a kibbutznik after all, was not having this. He pointed out that the factories were not always very economic and that it would quite suit the kibbutzniks to close some of them down instead of being benefactors who were reviled for being benefactors. Moreover, pay scales were higher, maybe by as much as 20 or 30 per cent, than in similar enterprises run by out-and-out capitalists.

By now we had arrived in Sderot. It was a dusty little place, befitting its claim to be the gateway to the Negev, Israel's southern desert. It was still Chanukah, the festival of lights, and, as anywhere else in Israel, little files of children were being led off on some suitably instructive outing. Coloured streamers were hung in the streets. We looked for the town hall, where we were to meet the mayor.

Old men, wearing fez-like headgear and holding dangerous-looking sticks, were sitting on benches berating each other. We asked where the town hall might be. Everyone knew, naturally, but no-one was able to tell us clearly how to get there. So we decided to park the car and, fighting our way through yet another file of children, began looking for this invisible municipal centre. A boy on a bicycle guided us, and a good thing too. We might never have found it for ourselves.

It was an unkempt building, which could have been anything from a small factory to a public lavatory. At a desk just inside the entrance sat an unshaven man who at first had neither knowledge of nor interest in us. Amram Luk, who after all had run a place like this, persisted, and suddenly this Sderot version of a municipal commissionaire decided that we had the right to be there. Signals were sent, and an official-looking person came down a flight of stone steps and herded us up them.

We passed tiny, cell-like offices, in which men in shirt-sleeves and woman in skirts and blouses were gossiping, and then were shown into a large, rectangular room, which came as quite a shock after the scruffiness and seediness we had seen so far. There were a large table and chairs which, though upon closer examination they turned out to be covered in plastic, could easily have passed for leather. This was elegance by any standard, and turned out to be Sderot's council chamber.

There we were met by a group of men. Standing out among them was a young man with a kind of Oriental-Afro hair-style. His sallow face was decorated by a massive black walrus moustache. His thickset frame was dressed in an open-necked shirt and pullover, and greenish corduroy trousers. Even though the voice in which he greeted us was incongruously high-pitched, his presence was commanding. This was Amir Peretz, mayor of Sderot for all of one year, a member of the Labour Party and, as I found out when I asked, 32 years old. He was Moroccan in origin, though born in Israel. The people with him were expert advisers who (when later they were allowed to speak, briefly) turned out to be mainly of Ashkenazi origin.

Once we were drinking and eating away, Amir Peretz began on us. He told us about Moroccans, just as Amram Luk had. Moroccans had come to Israel because the Land of Israel was the Jews' Mecca, and it was part of the Jewish religion to come and live in that land. However, for Orientals Israel was far from the Garden of Eden. He repeated Amram Luk's complaint that the socialistic kibbutz factory managers treated the employed proletariat in the way that capitalist bosses in other countries treat their workers. In fact, said Amir Peretz, the kibbutz capitalists were worse.

'In Sderot,' he declared, 'sixty per cent of the workers are employed by the kibbutzim in their regional enterprises. The kibbutzniks are trying to take total control of the labour market, to dominate it.'

Amir spoke in Hebrew and was interpreted by one of his advisers. Unlike Amram Luk, he had had neither the opportunity nor the need to learn English. He laid down the terms of discussion. Amram Luk conformed to others. Amir Peretz required others to conform to him.

At this point a telephone was heard ringing in another room, and an aide came in to call the mayor away. He was gone a few minutes and returned to announce in quite a casual manner that it had been the Prime Minister on the line. He wanted Sderot to join in some regional enterprise scheme, and needed Amir Peretz's opinion. It seemed that the mayor was agreeable but, as the conversation proceeded, I got the impression that co-operation, even with the Prime Minister, would, like everything else that Amir did, be on Amir's own terms.

His high voice now continued its tirade against the kibbutzim. Not long ago, he said, the workers of Sderot had gone on strike against the kibbutz managers – right-wing workers striking against socialistic employers; for the people of Sderot, he said, voted pro-Likud by two-to-one. The socialists brought in the police against the workers, and there was violence.

'We have capitalist employers as well, here in Sderot', said Amir, 'and you will see that they are more socially conscious than the kibbutz employers. The kibbutz managers do not give consideration to the dignity of the workers. They will not even allow their children to be educated with our children. They have their own schools and do not let us into them.'

Benny bridled beside me as Amir Peretz launched this indictment which, on the face of it, sounded very reasonable. I knew that later I would get the other side of the story, and I did. Benny pointed out that if the local schools merged with those of the kibbutzim and the government then eroded standards in those schools, or changed the curriculum, the kibbutzniks would lose while the townspeople would not gain.

Even now, while listening to him make his case, I could see for myself some flaws in what the mayor was saying. Whatever he thought about the kibbutzniks, they had undeniably brought employment to Sderot, and Sderot needed employment. It had 15 per cent unemployment and unemployment was getting worse all the time, in a town which was composed of Jews 70 per cent of whom were of North African origin, with the rest mainly from Romania. There was, however, now an even lower stratum, for Ethiopian Jews had come to settle in Sderot.

I saw some of these newcomers from Africa almost immediately. Our discussion over, Amir Peretz took me on a tour around his town and there on the streets walked these very black Jews. I was told that, when they had arrived, the country's Orthodox rabbis had refused to accept the Ethiopian men as Jews until they were properly circumcised. A circumcision operation was not in fact a practical proposition, since the men had already had their genitals docked and accordingly had nothing more that they could give. The rabbis suggested that a ceremonial shedding of a drop or two of blood would do as a symbolic substitute, but the Ethiopian males were indignant at any suggestion that their Judaism might be questioned and refused to co-operate. Now here they were, as we drove around Sderot, walking along, defiant and – rare in any conflict with Israel's powerful clergy – so far victorious and as intact bodily as when they had arrived in the country.

With the mayor driving us in his own car, we went off to the industrial estate, where the allegedly slave-driving kibbutzniks held sway. Our first call was to a chicken-slaughtering factory. I said, vehemently, that I did not wish to see the chickens slaughtered, and this refusal was accepted with some puzzlement by Amir. However, I was then introduced to the factory's resident engineer, a Jew of Argentinian origin called Ernesto. Never had he previously met anyone who had not been in a slaughterhouse. He was consumed with enthusiasm for slaughtering, and absolutely insisted that, if I refused to see the actual murder of these birds, I should at any rate inspect the factory's other operations.

There was no possibility of my refusing this pressing invitation, particularly since Ernesto confided in me that he voted Labour, yet another of the managerial class who was a socialist; I commented to him that Israel was the only country I knew where the bosses tried to persuade the workers to vote Labour, but he detected no incongruity. He made me put on a white coat, and in we went.

'They must kill a great many, every day,' I said.

'Yes,' replied Ernesto proudly. 'Twenty-four thousand every eight hours.' I calculated in my head that this meant three thousand an hour, which worked out at fifty every minute. And there they came along on an overhead line, moving relentlessly above me, trussed and stripped corpses of chickens being processed for the pot by happy, smiling women. Ernesto led me out, proudly informing me that these women each took home $500 a month after all deductions, and that this was up to 30 per cent above the going rate.

Amir Peretz now took charge of me again, and began to guide me around his town. As we drove along, the mayor, a highly effective and dedicated local politician, waved at everyone, and I noticed with a fellow-politician's interest that quite a lot of people waved at him, some of them indeed before he started the waving process. The recognition factor, as American sociologists would put it, was high. Old men in long robes, young women in housecoats, stood about in the streets. Because of the holiday, lots of children were running around. A tremendous proportion of the males, men and boys, wore skullcaps.

It was a lovely day in this awful little town. The benign sun shone out of a cloudless sky over the dingy multi-storey flats, covered with laundry. The sun shone, too, over houses which were being renovated. There were orange and lemon trees all over the place. Bougainvillea concealed some of the ugliest excrescences. Mayor Peretz was proud, and rightly so, of the renovation that was providing better homes as well as new homes. Still, despite the trees and the flowers and the renovation and the enthusiasm, Sderot was a dump, and the Moroccans had been sent to live in this dump.

As we drove around, and in between waves, I asked Amir about himself. He had had quite an adventurous past before settling down to life in a town where, like Amram Luk in Beit Shemesh, his obvious abilities had managed to get him

97

elected by Likud voters. He had even been a regular soldier and had served for a time as a parachutist. Now he lived in a small flat provided by the Jewish Agency, although he was having a new house built for himself. He pointed to this with pride as we drove past. It did not look like much of anything yet, but I had a feeling, after watching Amir as an operator, that it would be as much a show-house as was possible in Sderot and that next to this residence, at any rate, there would be none of the rubbish that was so casually deposited in other parts of town.

I asked Amir: 'How did you come to join the Labour Party and become active in it?'

His reply was prompt, if peculiar: 'It was after Labour lost the election in 1981 and so many Moroccans had voted for Likud. I wanted to show that Sephardis were not simply a pro-Likud herd.'

He had certainly shown that. I had rarely met a man who was less a member of anybody's herd. As an energetic and talented Sephardi, he had immense scarcity value in the Labour Party and was able, to a large extent, to make his own terms.

Now we were going to another industrial estate. This one was run by private enterprise. We first visited a small establishment where machines spewed forth concertina-like wads of paper especially manufactured for computer print-outs. The manager gave me a little gadget that combined a note-book with a credit-card-holder. It was certainly better than being given a dead chicken as a memento.

Our main call was at a spick-and-span little factory owned by a company named Spectronix. The company was about fifteen years old, but the branch in Sderot was rather newer. I did not have much hope of this visit. Small factories are all alike really, and I had been warned in advance that I would be made to watch a video-film about this establishment and its product, which was something to do with extinguishing systems.

I was taken round the factory which, unlike most Israeli industrial establishments, was spotlessly neat. It even had little boxes of plants stationed around the various shop floors.

It might almost have been in Japan. Then we went into a little room where the video display was waiting. It in fact turned out to be very interesting, since what Spectronix were making here was an extinguishing system for the crew cabins of armoured vehicles. It seemed that most injuries in tanks came from burns when the vehicles were hit and set on fire, and what Spectronix had invented was a mechanism which instantaneously turned itself on when a fire broke out in such circumstances. It had been adopted in the Israeli army and had already had a healthy effect on casualty figures in the Lebanon war, as various graphs convincingly demonstrated.

I said to Uri Levy, one of the senior managers there, that all this was highly impressive, but why had he and his colleagues come to out-of-the-way Sderot to do it?

'Well,' said Uri, 'partly it is because we are near to the University of Beersheba.' He hesitated, a little bashfully: 'But also it is out of Zionism. We want to help development in this place and provide jobs. Of course we got subsidies to come here as well. That was the policy when we had a Labour Government.'

I looked around the table, at dashing Uri and his less colourful but no doubt equally efficient fellow-managers and asked them what party they supported. All but Uri remained bashfully silent, but Uri himself said without quibble that he supported the Labour Party. Here was yet another manager, this time an unashamed profit-seeking (and profit-making) capitalist who voted socialist and employed Likud electors.

Amir had sat at the end of the table, with a lazy smile on his face, saying nothing and eating tangerines. I was beginning to see what he was up to. I saw even more as Uri told me about all the social projects that his little factory promoted in Sderot. He had one scheme for retarded children, another for the elderly. Then there was a children's computer club.

'Why do you do all these things?' I asked him.

He hesitated, somewhat bashfully, and replied: 'For idealism.'

No wonder Amir had brought me here. He wanted me

to see that the capitalists cared about their employees and their families, while the alleged socialists, the kibbutzim, used their enterprises to grind the faces of the workers. It was no matter to him that Uri, nice and charming and full of goodwill as he undoubtedly was, had scooped up government subsidies before building his clean, well-lighted factory ten years before, and was making very nice profits indeed, while the kibbutzim were actually incurring losses as a result of their decision to plant factories here. Amir was using the presence of Uri and other entrepreneurs like him to show up the kibbutzim, who were vulnerable precisely because everyone expected them to be socially motivated. He was playing off the socialists against the capitalists, and winning popularity among his voters as he did so. It was an exceptionally shrewd political ploy, and I was consumed with admiration for this adept, even cunning, young man.

Now I understood why Yehiel had insisted that I come to Sderot and meet Amir. Now I realized why he had arranged that Amram Luk should come with me.

Amram was the old kind of Israeli Oriental – an immigrant, decent, loyal, pliable, available to be used and exploited by the Labour establishment, ready to be palmed off as a token Sephardi with an unelectable 72nd place on the party's list of election candidates.

Amir was the new Moroccan. He had been born in Israel. He knew the score. Far from being pliable, he manipulated others. No-one was ever going to exploit him; if there was any exploiting, he was going to do it. The Labour Party, in its decline in support among the Sephardis, needed active, influential young Sephardis, needed him; and he was not going to trade himself at a bargain price. He was mayor already, far younger than when Amram had been elected in Beit Shemesh. Between him and the Labour establishment it was not a relationship of 'Don't call me, I'll call you.' Indeed, the Prime Minister did call him, and he took it for granted that that should be so. When he appeared on the Labour list of candidates, it would not be as Number 72. Amir was going to be much higher up. Amir was going to be elected. Amir, before he was done, was destined to be a Cabinet Minister.

The juxtaposition of Amram and Amir was like a Before and After advertisement. The two together – one tired though not particularly old, the other lively and thrusting; the one played out, the other with everything to go for – were a living commentary on Israeli social progress and social flux. They illustrated change in the Labour Party, in the Sephardi community, in the ethnic balance in Israeli society.

Amir was on the make, quite attractively so, but definitely on the make; moreover, barring some accident, he would make it. Amram was a figure of the past, charming, clever, rueful, knowing what had happened to him but unable and unwilling really to complain much about it.

Amran had never been, certainly now would never be, a danger to anyone. Amir was potentially very dangerous indeed. He had no obvious commitment to the Labour Party over and above the Labour Party's commitment to him. He had no compunction in challenging the kibbutzim, the very heart of the Israeli socialist dream. Down here in scruffy little Sderot, he regarded himself as much as a pioneer as any of those allegoric figures in those heroic frontier kibbutzim, and he was going to make sure that the proper recognition would come his way. If the Labour Party wanted Sephardi votes – and the Labour Party needed those votes desperately – then it was going to pay for them in recognition of people like Amir, and especially Amir himself.

On the way back, Benny and Amram Luk chatted a little in Hebrew, while I thought over what I had seen and heard. Then we all talked in English. Amram was perfectly conscious of what I had learned and the part he had played in my lesson. In the late winter afternoon, as a weak sun lit up the fields, he made it clear that he felt that, in his time and in his allotted place, he had fulfilled a role in the development of the state which he certainly did not regret and of which he was indeed properly proud.

We bowled up a little hill in Beit Shemesh and he expressed genuine regret that my timetable did not allow me to visit his home. He asked me, with obvious sincerity, to call on him if ever I was in the area again.

We dropped him off at the end of his street and, a bit tired, a bit bedraggled, very dignified, he turned a corner and disappeared from view. A whole segment of the history of Israel disappeared with him.

9

An Evening at Arye's

All over Israel, I met and spoke to all sorts of people. One meeting, organized by Yehiel in his office, was with people involved in Israeli television. They were raucous and argumentative and friendly. We did not talk about anything much, though we had a pleasant evening amicably quarrelling while, in the way of Israelis, they explained British politics to me. As we parted, one of them gave me a present. His name was Yigal Lossin, and he had played a major part in the production of a series on Israeli television that described the events leading to the founding of Israel. A book, a huge book, had been compiled from this series, and Yigal Lossin presented me with a copy. Naturally, I was grateful, but I was also unimpressed. After all, I had read about the foundation of Israel countless times. It was an old story to me.

I tore the cellophane wrapping off this volume, whose name was *Pillar of Fire*, and thought I would take a casual glance through its pages. From the moment I opened the book, I was transfixed. It contained thousands of pictures, some of great power. As the hours went by, and I turned page after page, I was, in turn, angered, uplifted, and moved. From time to time tears came to my eyes. Yes, it was certainly an old story that I was reading, but it did set into context everything that I had been seeing and hearing during this visit to Israel. It demonstrated more clearly than any political propagandist why there had to be an Israel, and what travails had preceded even the most controversial manifestations of the modern Israeli state.

Here were pictures of the pogrom in Kishinev, Russia, in 1903. An indecent jumble of torn Torah scrolls. A close-up of a dead baby, thrown out of an upper-storey window.

From Palestine, there were photographs of the Nebi Mussa riots of 1920 in Jerusalem, corpses of murdered Jews, a bearded old man and a child. And then again, pictures of the riots in Hebron in 1929, in which sixty-six Jews had been killed.

The photographs from Europe were the hardest to bear. Vienna, 1938: bearded Jews made to scrape the pavements while Nazi onlookers smirked. Warsaw, 1939: another bearded Jew, having his beard and side-curls cut off, a look of total resignation on his face. Another Jew, wearing a prayer shawl, forced to kneel in the street.

Russia, 1941: a German soldier shoots a Jewish woman holding her baby. Lvov, Poland: a truly horrible picture of a Jewish woman in her underwear being pursued shrieking through the streets. Latvia: naked Jewish women being shot. Auschwitz: a random pile of silently screaming Jewish corpses. The Warsaw Ghetto: an old bearded Jew, in a long coat, crawling in starvation along the pavement.

There were pictures of unwanted Jews, cast out from the civilized world. Scenes on board the ship, the *St Louis*, which sailed from Europe in 1939 with 930 Jews on board; they were prevented from landing in Cuba, in the United States, anywhere, and sent back to Europe. There was a smiling photograph of one of the passengers, Mr Fink, together with the information that he died in Auschwitz. More pictures, of another ship, the *Exodus 1947*, this time carrying 4,554 Jews. It got as far as the Palestine coast; its passengers, too, were sent back to Europe. Another photograph of Jews climbing the snow-covered Alps, hoping to make it to the Mediterranean for an attempt to enter Palestine illegally.

And two pictures of Jews who had made it to Palestine. One was of the founders of the Ein Harod settlement in 1924, using scythes to drain a water-logged swamp, the other of men who were permitted to serve in the British army, carrying a Torah scroll through the sands of the desert.

These photographs did not justify anything that was wrong

in the Israel of the 1980s, so long after the experiences they depicted. They *did* help to explain how most Israelis felt about their land. Other Israelis offered me more sophisticated explanations, some in fragmentary conversations, others in long discussions.

I went back to the Knesset. This time I did not go to the public floor, to the cafeteria with its blue table cloths, nor to the fifth floor with its party offices. This time I was ushered into the office of a committee chairman. It was quite grand, much more so than the rooms where I had met Aloni or even Eitan. I was to have a talk with Abba Eban.

The permutations of coalition-making had meant that there was no place in the government for the most eloquent Foreign Minister that Israel (or probably any other country) had ever had. Instead, he had been appointed Chairman of the Foreign Affairs and Defence Committee, as important a position as could be obtained outside the ranks of the Cabinet itself. Now, unbelievably, 69 years old, Eban sat regally behind his huge desk. We had known each other for years and greeted each other as fellow-authors, he, complacently, a best-seller.

He was bland, contented, but in another way very worried: 'We used to take democracy for granted in this country. Now it has to be inculcated. These things have to be taught.'

'Why', I asked, 'does democracy have to be taught all over again?'

'Because attitudes to government have changed. Criticism of the Likud government had lost its legitimacy.'

'Why?'

'They wrapped themselves in a flag.'

Eban shared the viewpoint that a student had expressed to me up on Mount Scopus: 'We have had a latent civil war. We became two nations. It was a conflict between the religious and the secular, the Sephardic and the Ashkenazi, the rich and the poor, the educated and the uneducated.'

In this comfortable room, then, the outlook did not seem so bright, even to a man who had endured all the perils of the birth of the state.

I met a woman called Dr Susan Hattis Rolef, an Ashkenazi with an American accent, who had written an interesting article in the *Jerusalem Post*. She was described there as a researcher and lecturer 'closely associated with the Labour Party'. Her article said, in part: 'Democracy in Israel is like the weather in England – everybody talks about it, and nobody seems to be doing anything about it. Democracy is much talked about because certain persons and bodies have found it opportune to re-emphasize anti-democratic values and principles in Judaism, which evolved hundreds of years ago to deal with circumstances that are no longer relevant. There are, thankfully, many rabbis who cherish democratic values, and they will have to contend with this problem.'

When I read this, my attention had been grasped because it seemed to me that Dr Rolef was dealing with the issues in Professor Tal's lecture that had so alarmed me. I read on with especial interest: 'The more pressing manifestations of the problem are two in number. The first stems from the belief of many people that Israel's democratic system can't cope effectively with the horrendous difficulties facing the state, especially on the economic plane. People express doubt about whether democracy is, after all, something worth treasuring.

'The most disconcerting aspect of this attitude is that those who should know better seem to believe that it is possible to have temporarily an enlightened dictator at the helm (everybody assumes that he *will* be enlightened), who will graciously give up his absolute powers after resolving Israel's urgent problems with a sweep of his magic wand.

'The second manifestation of the problem is the apparent belief of many youngsters and adults that even if democracy is a desirable system for the Jews in Israel, when it comes to dealing with the Arabs – whether inside the Green Line [post-1948 Israel's borders until the Six-Day War] or in the occupied territories – other principles, which have nothing in common with democracy, should dictate Israel's conduct.'

The problem was, as Dr Rolef explained to me over a kebab and hot oriental salad, that even those who claimed to believe in democracy did not necessarily share the same definition of it. Her article made a similar point that values 'promoted' differed widely: 'It seems that most of the politically affiliated bodies currently engaged in "promoting" democracy are associated with the Labour Movement. Other politically affiliated bodies engaged in educational activities seem more concerned with promoting Judaism and love for Greater Israel. In terms of efforts to strengthen democracy, this is disturbing.

'Youngsters are getting the impression that "democracy" is a vested interest of the Labour Movement, and that if they happen to sympathize with the Likud, or parties to the Likud's right, they may conclude that if the Labour Movement is so interested in democracy, perhaps democracy is somehow "unpatriotic."'

Still, she said, some agencies were making an effort: 'The new Knesset Speaker, Shlomo Hillel, is in the process of setting up a national council, of academics and intellectuals on the one hand, and of representatives of the educational establishment, the army and the media on the other, to make practical proposals as to how Israel's democratic roots can be strengthened.

'The Ministry of Education, especially since Yitzhak Navon became minister, has been giving the subject much thought. Dr Arik Karmon of Tel Aviv University, who was recently appointed to head a committee of experts to deal with democracy in the education system, says there are three spheres of activity for his committee. The first concerns immediate steps to combat the problem of Kahanism; the second concerns democracy as a central theme to be dealt with in the school system; and the third concerns long-term, comprehensive programmes on democracy, which would operate from kindergarten through twelfth grade and on into the army.'

A few days later, I picked up a copy of the *Jerusalem Post*. It reported an exchange in the Knesset. 'Education Minister Yitzhak Navon announced yesterday that his ministry had decide to make "education for democracy" the main home-room subject for the two years beginning September 1985.

'Navon was replying to a motion for the agenda by Chaike Grossman (Mapam), who said that it is vital to curb "the devil of racism and nationalism that is to be found in each one of us".

'For some time, Navon said, the ministry had been aware of tendencies of growing extremism, intolerance, and unconcern for the democratic system among many young people.

'Part of the education-for-democracy curriculum will aim to foster understanding and co-existence between Jews and Arabs, Navon said.

' "There are Jews who don't want a single Arab here", he said, "and Arabs whose aim is that not a single Jew shall be here. But there's nothing they can do about it; it is our destiny to live together. And the educational system is assuming the task of seeing to it that relations shall be positive and fruitful." '

That all seemed straightforward. I knew enough of Israel, however, to be aware that matters inevitably were much more complicated than that. I also knew that the best person in Israel to unravel and explain such complicated matters was Dan ('Dindush') Horovitz, the Professor of Political Science at the Hebrew University and, among brilliant academics, perhaps the most brilliant of them all. I had met him – and his father, a masterly Governor of the Bank of Israel – when I had first come to Israel nearly a quarter of a century before, and had kept in touch from time to time. Of course, he was an Ashkenazi. Now I rang the bell of his apartment in Tchernikovsky Street, a broad thoroughfare in a pleasant part of West Jerusalem.

Like Eitan, Horowitz outlined his terms of reference in tabular form: 'The problems are these:

1. Economic insecurity.
2. Loss of trust in the capacity of the democratic system to solve problems.
3. Combination of nationalism and religious fanaticism.
4. Populism – compensation by Orientals for social depri-

vation and a way of dissociating themselves from Arabs by associating themselves with radical nationalism.'

'Everything', said Dindush, 'is ripe for the appearance of fascism. This situation is exacerbated by the feeling that Arik Sharon is someone you have to fear. And people are afraid of the consequences of not joining him. A band wagon effect is being created.'

'Is it as dangerous as that?' I asked.

Dindush considered. 'Well,' he said pensively, 'he is a gambler and might make a mistake.'

What was the nature of Sharon's challenge?

'Any fascist leader identifies his own fortunes with those of the state.'

My mind immediately went to Sharon's libel action against *Time* magazine, which was then current and which Sharon was shortly to lose. In that legal case, Sharon had claimed that what *Time* had said about himself and the Sabra-Shatilla massacre was a blood libel on the whole Jewish people.

What I wanted to know was why Dindush believed that fascism was a threat at all in a country like Israel, with all its democratic traditions.

'The system is not strong enough to carry the problems.'

'But why Sharon? Why not someone else?'

'Kahane and Eitan are not sophisticated enough. Yet people want a strong personality to deliver the goods. For such a movement to succeed you need someone to combine the religious fanatics and the mob.'

'Why the religious fanatics? What role do they play?'

'You can't have a movement without an ideological elite and without zeal. Gush Emunim provide this.'

Dindush went on to expound his case by offering a compelling argument which I had never heard of before: 'There is a vacuum in the system which is being filled by religious fanaticism. When Ben-Gurion was Prime Minister, his achievement was to transform communal conflict into conflict between states, between Israel and the Arab nations.'

That, I understood, meant that potential conflict within Israeli society was externalized, with hostile Arabs seen as the adversary.

'But a change came. 1967 – the Six-Day War and the conquest of territories – started it. Communal conflict, over the control of these territories, was reintroduced into the system. What we were getting was tribal conflict, and that is Kahane's approach.'

Then the culmination came, with the Yom Kippur War in 1973, the war Israel started off by losing: 'The 1973 war brought about the breakdown of the old mystique of the dominant party, because of the loss of trust and confidence in Israel as a success story. It was that war, and its consequences, which brought the Likud to power in 1977. Demographic developments would have brought the Likud to power in the 1990s. The Yom Kippur War advanced the timetable.'

Then Dindush told me something that was amazing and paradoxical, but absolutely convincing: 'It was the signing of the peace treaty with Egypt that is responsible for the communal conflict within Israel. That peace treaty was Begin's achievement. Labour could never have done it. But by taking the pressure off the Egyptian front, it led to concentration on the West Bank, and consequently to the conflict about what we should do about it.'

Coupled with this development was the inadequacy of the machinery of government as it operated under the democratic process: 'It's a general deterioration of the system as a system for fulfilling the hopes of the people. For example, they solved the housing problem by creating slums.'

I took it that he meant new housing projects that deteriorated fast, or maybe were even inadequate to begin with; the same process that took place in Britain too and led to the alienation of the inner-city dwellers who in social and income terms are Britain's equivalent of the deprived Sephardis.

'It's the same with education. And then there are jobs. We have full employment, sure, but certain people, especially Orientals, are concentrated in occupations of lower prestige.

'So we have solved the problems technically. We have taken action on all of them. But we have not solved them essentially.'

What I had been learning from Dindush was that Israel

had all the problems of Western developed societies, together with an internal ethnic divide, plus, on top of it all, unique conflicts brought about by its geographical and military situation. No wonder that some people were turning to extreme solutions, fanned by religious ideologists who claimed, plausibly to many, that the solutions were in any case written in the Bible for all to see.

I left Jerusalem and travelled to Tel Aviv and went for the evening to Arye's house. Arye is a prosperous businessman. He owns a nice house, in a nice, northern, suburb of Tel Aviv. Approaching, I saw that it had a two-car entrance. It was a large, open-plan dwelling, with a tree growing dramatically and attractively through the middle of the interior. Everything about this place, in fact, was perfect. Arye, dark, handsome, with heavy features, had picked me up at my hotel. Now he introduced me to his wife Annette, born in France, blond and pretty. They made a picture-book couple in a picture-book house. They were almost too good to be true.

The dinner table was laid, beautifully, and a few minutes later Arye's brother, Yigal, a doctor, and his sister-in-law, Pamela, an immigrant from England, arrived. We sat down to dinner, and Annette served a model meal: a heavy vegetable soup, then chicken with petits pois and carrots, followed by a light salad. We talked, idly, about the kind of trivial topics that are discussed at any pleasant, friendly dinner-table in any country in the developed world.

Then the bell rang, and guests began to arrive. We moved from the dining section to a large, lower level with a sofa and comfortable chairs. Annette had disappeared at the end of dinner, and now a central table was full of bowls of nuts, dishes of sliced orange segments, and plates of cakes.

I shall not give the real names of the people who came, but endow them with artificial ones, as I have with Arye and Annette. So let us call the first arrival Gidi. He was the archetypal Israeli blond, and he turned up with his wife, Sarah, who was dark and pretty. Then came Moshe, who was an employee of the Labour Party, thin and moustached,

with his wife, Miriam, a small, dark woman, also a Labour
Party official. The men were all simply dressed in open-
necked shirts and slacks or corduroys; this made me feel
a fool, since I had put on a jacket and tie, believing I had
been invited to a formal occasion. I should have learned
by now that in Israel it is never a social error for a man
to dress informally. The women, on the other hand, as well
as being very attractive, were all extremely elegantly turned
out. About a dozen people assembled all told, but some of
them remained silent throughout. The most vocal women
were Arye's English-born sister-in-law, Pamela, and Esther,
a sturdy girl with sparkling eyes who was the only person
present proudly (if defiantly) to proclaim that she had voted
for the Likud. It was indeed symptomatic of all I had learned
in my time in Israel that this collection of attractive, prosperous, middle-class people, most of them so far as I could
tell in their early thirties, were Labour voters. All of them,
it goes without saying, were Ashkenazis, except for Arye,
who claimed to be a Sephardi on the grounds that his parents
had been born in Bulgaria. I was not sure exactly what he
had in common with, say, a labourer who had immigrated
from Morocco apart from their shared Jewishness.

This was a social evening, but all present knew that they
had been invited so that I could sound out their opinions.
I started them off by asking all present, as I had asked Shulamit Aloni, what had gone wrong. It is possible that, if I
had started by asking what was right with Israel, I might
have been given different answers; but somehow I doubt
it.

Gidi (a Labour voter) announced that he was fearful that
Sharon would become Prime Minister and endanger democracy, though he was not too precise about how this would
come about.

Moshe agreed. But Menahem, a successful businessman,
was not worried. 'Israel *needs* a dictatorship,' he insisted,
deliberately provocative, 'for four years or so, to clear up
problems that democratic leaders cannot cope with. I lived
for a while in Singapore. We need something like that.'

'Why', I asked, 'do you believe that a dictator will come

up with solutions that have evaded democrats? And why do you believe that a dictator will stop dictating at the end of four years? Maybe he will have got a taste for being dictator?'

Menahem did not reply. Avram then had his say. He was a typical argumentative Israeli, more anxious to provoke and annoy (in a pleasant way) than to conduct an argument. He stated flatly that he did not believe Israeli democracy to be in any danger at all.

Others joined in, all giving their views about the prospects for democracy. Apart from Avram, over the room as a whole there was an uncertainty about the future of democracy, but also an unwillingness to come to grips with what the problem for democracy really was.

So I switched the subject to the Lebanon war, and here again there was confusion. There was a surprising tendency not to decry just this war as an isolated event, but to be uncertain about the justice and clarity of purpose of any Israeli war except for the Six-Day War. Gidi spoke: 'The Six-Day War was a war to make everyone proud and hold their heads high.'

Even the Yom Kippur War was regarded with distaste by many of those present. These, I decided as I looked about the room, were not martial Israelis. On the other hand, they were increasingly unrepresentative of the country which they had become used to running and whose material benefits they enjoyed disproportionately.

On one matter they were, however, completely united. When I said that Israel had turned the occupied West Bank into a Bantustan, almost all of them descended on me in good-natured fury.

'What are we to do?' asked Dov, another businessman. 'We cannot give the Arabs civil rights. They are our enemies.'

Even Gidi, whom I had thought of as the most liberal among them, was indignant. 'The Arabs are doing fine, any-how,' he snorted.

Avran asserted that the only bad areas were the refugee camps, which he tried to discuss at length.

I interrupted to describe my experiences in Berka. Nobody was impressed. Despite what I told them, the assembled company were of the general view that Berka was better-off compared with what it had known under Jordanian rule.

'But that is not the comparison,' I said. 'Are the people of Berka better-off compared with you? Ought not that to worry you?'

Menahem then asked me the question I knew I would get at some point, the question first put to me by Levi Eshkol when he was Prime Minister: 'Why has Israel to be judged by standards different from those in other countries? After all, there is torture in Malaysia, there is torture in Syria.'

'Come off it,' I replied. I was as used to answering this question as I was to being asked it. 'Israel has to be judged by higher standards because she claims higher standards. If you want to be compared with Malaysia and Syria, fine, fair enough. No-one will expect anything of you. But the fact is that you don't want to be compared with those countries. You want to be compared with advanced Western democracies.'

There was a babble. Then our host, Ayre, who had not so far taken part in the discussion, interrupted. 'The problem is', he said, 'that Israeli youth has grown up with the West Bank as part of Israel. To them the pre-1967 borders, which we were always penned inside, do not exist.'

This was a most impressive statement. I recalled that recently I had been given a colourful little booklet, produced by the Israel Information Centre. On it a map of the whole of Palestine, including not only the West Bank and Gaza but even the Golan Heights, was included as part of Israel, without even a dotted line to separate out the Occupied Territories.

Arye went on, compellingly: 'Israeli youth are not like us. They have not grown up with the assumptions and experiences of Israelis of our age. They can drive wherever they want to. They take it for granted that a million Arabs are part of their state. They take it for granted that these Arabs have lower standards. They take it for granted that these Arabs do not have civil rights. They take it for granted that these Arabs do the menial jobs. All this seems to them the natural state of affairs and it colours their attitude towards

Arabs and towards democracy.'

These were devastating words. The ideal of Zionism had been that the Jews did all the jobs, the lot of them, from governing the country to cleaning the streets. Now the occupation of the West Bank was seen to have eroded the practice and therefore the principles of Zionism.

Everyone was sobered up by Arye's words. I do not mean that they had been affected by strong drink. This being a gathering of Israeli Jews, the intake of alcohol had been almost non-existent. But all who had been taking part in the discussion now had to admit that every Israeli under the age of twenty had a different Israel in his head than they had. It came home to them brutally that to these younger Israelis all the questions of frontiers, of settlements, of security, were quite different from what they were even to themselves, their elder brothers and sisters, gathered there at Arye's house.

Once again, as so often during my time in Israel, the issue of education was seen to be absolutely primary. The attitude of the young people would be fundamental in determining what kind of Israel was going to confront the remainder of the century, what view of democracy was going to prevail in this indispensable but tormented land. Regardless of wars with Arab neighbours, the battle for the future of Israel was going to be fought and won – or lost – in its army's educational units and in its schools.

The party broke up. People rose from their seats, ready to go home and prepare for another day. It was nearly 1 a.m. We had been talking for hours. One by one each of the guests, regardless of what they had said in discussion, however heated their attitude had been, came to me and with great genuineness wished me good fortune.

In the way that happens when a party is ending, I had brief, private conversations with several of my companions of the evening. My host, Arye, confided that his mother, who had come from Bulgaria in 1948, had told him that she would leave the country if Sharon became Prime Minister. His instinct was the same, he said. He added that, of course, in the end neither of them would leave Israel for any reason; but that was the way they felt.

Moshe agreed with me that an evening of tormented discussion about the very nature of Israel would have been inconceivable in such a gathering ten years ago.

Yigal detached me from the rest and said to me, with great deliberation and earnestness: 'Hold to your views. The Jews outside Israel have a duty to speak their minds to Israeli Jews.'

10

Blintzes in Lebanon

It was 7 a.m. when I arrived at Sde Dov, not a good time of the day for me at all. I had on many occasions flown from Sde Dov, the military airfield just north of the suburbs of Tel Aviv, dangerously sited next to the chimneys of the Reading D power station. I had taken off from there for the Gaza Strip just after the Six-Day War. It had several times been my starting point to Sinai, where on a memorable occasion one engine of our twin-engined 'plane ceased functioning and we flew carefully over a straight road through the desert until we managed, just in time, to land at El Arish.

Now, for the first time, I was about to fly from Sde Dov to a war, to the Israeli-occupied area of Lebanon, where almost every day Israeli soldiers were being killed or wounded by mines or bombs or ambushes.

A few days after I made this trip, the Israeli government announced its decision to withdraw its armed forces from Lebanon. A couple of months after that the protracted, humiliating and horrifyingly blood-soaked withdrawal was actually in process. That withdrawal, with its savage and meaningless and purposeless deaths on both sides, brought to a head the self-doubt and repugnance that many Israelis had felt about the whole Lebanon imbroglio.

The self-doubt had been stated most bitterly in an article in the Israeli daily paper *Ha'aretz* by a staff member whose son was serving in Lebanon. This man wrote: 'On the radio you hear about "four attempted attacks" and you think of him there in the cold, lying in a fox-hole and looking around him in dread; from which direction will the rocket-propelled grenade, or the round of bullets, or the bomb come? When several news bulletins go by without a word about Lebanon, you are scared that something has happened and they have not had time yet to notify their families . . .

'The one who should not be there, the one who should not have been there from the start is my son; the son whom they have turned into a "liberator of Lebanon", who changes the order of creation, makes the Phalange rulers, and establishes a new order. Now hated, loathed, isolated and scared, he is a living target whose entire national mission is to protect himself . . .

'He, my son, is there, while I – a member of the trembling minority – face the telephone, the radio, and the doorbell, my new enemies at home.'

Israeli parents had always, in other wars, worried quite naturally about the safety of their sons in battle. No-one had ever translated his worry into such a frantic outpouring as this.

The repugnance about Lebanon was demonstrated to me when, after my return from my trip there, I spent an evening with an acquaintance, Mouli, and some of his friends. They asked me with interest what I had thought of the country. I said it was beautiful. Several of them said they had done their reserve service there, and one of them went on: 'Yes, I thought it was beautiful too. But I spent too much of my time looking down, in case there were mines.'

The others nodded. I was filled with shame at my unthinking tourist's enthusiasm. I had fully realized, of course, that military service must have its frightening times. Never before, however, had I heard Israelis admit in this naked way to being afraid.

Lebanon was an unprecedented trauma for Israel, which was why I had felt it essential to go and see for myself. I had in fact had a bit of difficulty arranging this visit to Lebanon, not because of the dangers which, after all, were my look-out, but because someone somewhere in authority regarded me as unreliable. An article about developments in Israel that I had written in a British magazine was felt to be unhelpful, and certain meetings and facilities were accordingly being denied to me: rather silly, really, since such lack of co-operation could scarcely be likely to make me more friendly. When I had told my contact in the Foreign Office in Jerusalem – a link helpfully arranged for me by the Embassy in London – that I wanted to visit Lebanon while parts of it were still occupied by the Israelis, there was silence for a few days.

Then I was notified to be available on a certain date at Kiryat Shmona, right in the northernmost part of Israel, where I should book myself in at an hotel and where the following day the Israeli army would come and collect me. A very nice programme had been arranged for me, and I would be spending my time with various elements in the South Lebanon fighting forces.

That arrangement seemed just about acceptable to me, though I was somewhat peeved that I was to be dumped among the South Lebanese soldiers rather than with the Israelis. It was, after all, one of the prime purposes of my expedition to talk to Israeli soldiers in Lebanon about what they were doing in that country and how they felt about the war and the prolonged occupation.

The South Lebanese army was just one of the shifting kaleidoscope of groupings which made it difficult, if not downright impossible, for an outsider to understand what was going on in that country whose population was divided between Moslems and Christians, with further divisions within these religious groupings creating almost hopeless confusion. The Christians were divided between Greek Orthodox, Greek Catholic and Maronite, of whom the Maronites were the strongest. It was they who provided their country with its presidential family, the Gemayels, and who made up the savage militia, the Phalange, who had been responsible for the horrifying massacre in the Sabra and Shatilla refugee camps. They too provided the commanders of the South Lebanese army, Mayor Saad Haddad and, when he died (surprisingly, of natural causes) in 1984, his successor, Major-General Antoine Lahd.

Most members of the South Lebanese army were Maronite

Christians, though Lahd claimed that a substantial minority were Moslems. In any case, this army, if it could be called such, was a curious band of men. Its numbers were imprecise, estimates ranging from 500 to 2,000 and more. Some of its soldiers wore Phalange uniforms, others the uniform of the Republic of Lebanon's official army (such as that was) and others still uniforms provided by the Israelis, which closely resembled those supplied to Israeli soldiers themselves. The Israelis certainly trained, paid and supplied the South Lebanese force, and looked to it to police the area north of the international border after the Israel Defence Forces had withdrawn. On the other hand, the Israelis had no real confidence in the South Lebanese, one senior Israeli officer declaring that they 'couldn't even fight a cripple'. Furthermore, Lahd for his part avowed no particular loyalty to the Israelis, and made it clear that he wanted them out of his country.

This was a sentiment shared by the different groups of Moslems, themselves all split internally. The Palestinians, of course, were not Lebanese at all, and their principal military and political wing, the Palestine Liberation Organization, had been chased out of the country – at any rate as an effective fighting force – by the Israelis. That left the three indigenous Lebanese groups who, however, like all Moslems, were local offshoots of much larger sects straddling several countries throughout Islam. The Lebanese Druzes – or some of them, for they too were split – were a troublesome lot to the Israelis, unlike the Druzes of Israel, the only Moslems permitted to serve in the Israel Defence Forces. The Druzes are a splinter which broke away from a bigger splinter of the Shi'ite Moslems, centuries ago, and now practice an extremely recondite faith.

Among the more conventional Moslems, the Sunnis outnumber the Shi'ites, in Lebanon, just as they do in Islam as a whole. The Sunnis – split between conservative elders and a younger generation associated somewhat with the Palestinians but not too happy with them either – were the more prosperous and provided more of the establishment among the Lebanese Moslem community. They do not go in for priests and Imams, unlike the Shi'ites, who share the faith of the Iranian Moslems and are accordingly sympathetic to Ayatollah Khomeini. The Shi'ites, poorer and less well educated than the Sunnis, achieved greater prominence than their co-religionists both because their population was more heavily concentrated in the south of Lebanon, where the fighting was fiercest, and because they had their own militia, the Amal. Furthermore, from time to time the Israelis, justifiably lacking confidence in the South Lebanese Army, looked wistfully to the Amal as a possible ally in policing the border area. Yet, again paradoxically, it was the Israeli imprisonment of more than 700 Shi'ites that was to lead in June 1985 to the hijacking of a TWA aircraft and to a further Israeli humiliation in having to agree (on behalf of the Americans) to yield to terrorists by eventually freeing all of these prisoners in order to achieve the liberation of American hijack hostages.

Lebanon was a maelstrom, and the Israelis must have incessantly cursed themselves for becoming involved in its mind-bogglingly complicated tangle of military, political and, above all, religious alliances and – more reliable by far – enmities. No wonder they regarded my wish to have a look at the country as a further, if minuscule, burden that they could well do without. I was a bother, and they soon made that clear. I received a further telephone call from the Foreign Office instructing me to hire a car to take me into Lebanon, and of such a kind – either four-door or four-wheel-drive, though which of the two was not made absolutely clear – as to enable the Israeli forces to provide me with reliable security; or, at any rate, with security that was as reliable as could be achieved in that lethal snake-pit. I was baffled, not to say put out, that I was being asked to act as a kind of Hertz agency for the Israeli army, and told my contact that I did not really regard these proposals as what I had in mind. Perhaps the best thing would be for me to discuss them with the Minister of Defence, Yitzhak Rabin, my old adversary at the time of the Six-Day War, whom I was due to see in a couple of days and whom I could ask whether I should bring my own sandwiches as well.

At this point a friend of mine in the Knesset, Ora Namir, telephoned to ask how I was getting on. I described my

Lebanon problem and she exploded with fury. Within a few hours, my Foreign Office contact was back on the line. By a happy coincidence, a helicopter was going to Lebanon the day after next, and if I cared to join it I could spend an interesting day with the Israeli Army.

That, then, was how I came to find myself at Sde Dov one winter morning. The security, as usual in Israel, appeared to be chaotic. Nobody in the huts at the airfield's entrance seemed to be expecting me, or to know where I ought to go. Nevertheless, after various telephone calls conducted by a bespectacled young female soldier who put down her knitting in order to make them, I was directed to another hut. Inside this hut sat a second girl, again bespectacled but this time not knitting. She industriously marked me off on a sheet on a clipboard. I was then told to sit down on a sofa and, this being Israel, was instantly offered refreshment.

I waited, wondering if anything in particular was going to happen or whether I would just be left to sit there for the rest of the day. People did start coming in, one of them, I was later told, an officer who had asked to be released from the armed forces because of his opposition to the Lebanon war. He, plus all of the others, completely ignored me. They all seemed much preoccupied, were dressed in a variety of military outfits, and kept walking in and out of the hut. All, without exception, accepted coffee and chocolate coconut cake from the woman orderly who, like all women in the allegedly egalitarian Israeli services, seemed to have been allotted a place very much in the home. They conversed with each other in a jocular manner, and one of them made a half-hearted and not very successful attempt to polish his boots. He was the first Israeli serviceman I had ever seen who appeared in any way conscious of his appearance.

Finally, however, I was recognized, or at any rate acknowledged, and at 7.45 a.m. with my travelling companions, mainly senior serviceman, I trooped out of the hut along to the airfield, and into a Cessna 'plane which, just inside the door, had pasted a special Prayer for the Flight. Nobody recited it, but I felt somewhat comforted by its very presence. We took off and swung out over the sea. The ugly towers of Tel Aviv rose quite bewitchingly out of the morning mist of what had turned into a lovely winter day. We flew along the coast, over the hotels of the resort of Herzliyya with their blue, lozenge-shaped swimming pools, and then swung inland.

Below us was the green land of Israel. Its fields, ploughed and cultivated to within an inch of their lives, were discernible in neat rectangles. Tiny settlements and their orchards glistened in the sunlight. To our left, all white with more tower blocks, was the resort town of Natanya. We turned to the north-east and now, on the right, in the haze loomed the hills of Samaria on the West Bank. On the left I could see the new power station at Hadera, coal-fired, and with a jetty to receive the coal that was imported from Britain. Thin white cloud rolled under us and when it drifted away I saw that we were over hills, and that the prospect had become much more rugged. On the hilltops were Arab towns and Jewish settlements, each easily distinguishable from the other. The Arab towns were white and sprawled untidily. The Jewish settlements were, as usual, crowned with red roofs.

Mount Carmel was on the left, with Haifa barely visible. Immediately below was Megiddo, the site of Armageddon, as one of the escorting officers bawled to me over the drilling sound of the engine. Below the distant Mount Hermon, where Israel, Lebanon and Syria meet, the hills swooped down in an escarpment to the preternatural green of the Valley of Jezreel. Ahead of us, on a hilltop, sat Arab Nazareth and, tumbling down the hillside, the tower blocks of the newer, Jewish part of the town. Fishponds gleamed. Perched on a mountain, again all white, was the Jewish holy town of Safad. Nearby was Jethro's Tomb. Beyond was Tiberias, on the Sea of Galilee.

The huge lake really was shaped like a harp, explaining why the Israelis call it Kinneret, the Hebrew word for that instrument. The water was blinding when the sun caught it and blazed a dazzling path along it. Slight winds scored stippled patterns on its surface. The fishing boats, which catch the St Peter's Fish that can be eaten in what pass in Israel for smart restaurants, traced herring-bone designs behind them. Here was the mountain where the Sermon on the Mount was preached, there the place – Tabgha – where Jesus performed the miracle of the loaves and fishes. Sited above was a huge and imposing Christian church, down below were the remains of a tiny synagogue. On the left was the National Water Carrier, the pipeline that carries water from the fertile North to the parched Negev in the South. On the right was the grimness of the Golan Heights, towering above Israeli settlements such as the beautifully afforested Kfar Hanassi. Not a cultivable square inch was left untouched. If my Israeli hosts had deliberately set out to show me all that their nation had achieved, all that they were seeking to defend, all that their name for the Lebanon invasion, Operation Peace for Galilee, was meant to safe-guard, they could not have done it more effectively.

We landed at Machanayim, an airstrip near Rosh Pinna, three miles west of the River Jordan where it met the Golan Heights. It was still not quite 8.20 a.m. Once the Cessna's engines came to a halt, it was so quiet that I could hear the birds singing. A helicopter was waiting, a seven-seater. We were strapped in. Earphones were attached to our heads, so that we could communicate over the din made by the machine in motion. This time we were on our way to Lebanon itself, and I noted with relief that our conveyance was also sanctified with a Prayer pasted to it. Music came in over the earphones, broadcast by the Israeli Forces' radio station. Now we had been joined by a general, a large man, chubby but not fat, disconcertingly young as is always the case with senior Israeli officers. His name was Yomtov, and he was the boss hereabouts. At 8.38 a.m. we took off.

Mount Hermon, which it was impossible really to lose sight of, was a dim wrinkle to our right. Below were the pines of green and leafy Metulla, the most northerly town in Israel. On the right was the Huleh Valley, once a swamp, since drained. It was now intensively cultivated with orchards, looking as though they had been painted by a child, and also contained a nature reserve dense with water birds, some of which could be seen perched by pools. On the right were the Golan Heights. Ahead was a settlement which I was told over the crackling earphones had been a target for rockets until Operation Peace for Galilee had cleared away the Palestine Liberation Organization. Below us were the low, hangar-like buildings of an industrial zone, together with a sports field and swimming pool.

We landed in a rather scrubby vacant spot in Metulla, guided in by a smoke flare. A villainous-looking reception party awaited us, just short of slovenly, as Israeli troops generally are, and all armed to the teeth. We were joined here by a young bespectacled woman who was revealed to be a Major in rank and who was introduced to me as a newly appointed military spokesman for the area. We all got into a white Ford Granada, which, too, contained a Prayer for the Journey. A command car followed us. The border commander drove. We left Metulla, despite a large sign which pleaded: 'Come back soon!'

With the foothills of Hermon on our right and the sky decorated with mottled cloud, we were zipping along one of the Israeli Army's main entrances to Lebanon. Our destination was clarified by a notice in Hebrew, white on green, which read: 'To Lebanon only'. Within minutes we arrived in an enormous military car park, a marshalling area. Dozens of trucks were drawn up, their sides open, the soldiers in them sitting back to back, looking outward, so that they were in a position to shoot without delay. This was where the men going into Lebanon checked out. No-one could enter without permission; everyone had to be personally registered. This was not an army of occupation or of administration. This was an army actively at war.

As so often with Israelis, apparent confusion concealed meticulous organization. We crossed the border at 9.06 a.m. Behind us was a jeep, with a gum-chewing soldier – Israelis are always eating – holding a gun at the ready. We were escorted by a Military Police command car. We were now going through the Marjayun Valley. An olive grove was on our left. Another checkpoint loomed. The soldiers here were well wrapped up against what could be a fierce Lebanon winter, though, happily, today was mild. We drove through the town of Marjayun itself, headquarters of the late Major

Haddad's South Lebanese Army, and went past a large, isolated house labelled optimistically Voice of Hope. This had been intended as a radio station broadcasting propaganda for Haddad. I was informed that Marjayun had been deserted when the PLO were in control, but that now inhabitants were returning.

I looked around me. The fields were cultivated, but seemed scruffy compared to the almost manicured state of their Israeli counterparts. On some houses, washing was drying in the quite benevolent breeze. A plump cow was tethered to a tree. The houses appeared jerry-built, made of cement and sand, but most of them seemed to be topped with television aerials.

We sped through a Christian village. Women, clearly well-fed, and well-dressed in coats topped with fur, strolled along. Children larked about. A little fruit stall waited for customers. Then the commander pointed to a great ridge on the right. Sprouting out of it, as if growing naturally, was a huge fortress like something out of Walt Disney. This, I was told, was Beaufort, a Crusader castle. I said I thought it was beautiful. I was promptly told that it had been used by the PLO for firing shells into Israel. A herd of goats, mobbing us, did not seem to care either way.

We were now on a road 2,000 feet high. There were massive signs of the Israeli military presence. A convoy lumbered along. On the left was a former British military airfield, left over from the First World War, now cultivated untidily like a patchwork quilt made by a very old lady with poor eyesight. All around us, houses were going up. The war had interrupted their progress but not stopped it. We went through another village. This was large enough for an ambitious commercial establishment, a men's barber shop proudly sign-posted: 'Salon Hilton Pour Hommes'. Another village clung to a hillside, looking unreal, more like a primitive painting.

Then, suddenly, we were back at the international border. We had been going due south and now we arrived at a fence, menacingly electrified and manned by South Lebanese troops who looked scarcely into their teens. Security here was very tight. A car bomb had exploded not long ago, and special precautions were now taken. The Israelis, I was informed, bought nothing in Lebanon. 'Not even a cold drink?' I asked incredulously 'No,' I was told firmly, 'it begins with Coca-Cola and ends with drugs.' However, Lebanese were allowed across the frontier to make purchases. 'They actually buy flowers in Israel,' I was told.

'Cut flowers?'

'Yes. There is a lot of funerals in Lebanon. They need flowers.'

We had paused before entering the border point and I took the opportunity of questioning Ofra, the military spokesman. I asked her what her attitude was to the Lebanese campaign.

'No question that we had to go in,' she replied. 'The question was, how far?'

'What do *you* think?'

'As someone whose best friend was killed, it's difficult for me to say.'

Embarrassed, I changed the subject and asked her if, as a woman, she minded constantly being referred to as a spokes-*man*. Her reply was just as doleful: 'I don't want equal rights. I don't want to kill.'

We drove through the border checkpoint, past a bank thoughtfully provided for traders, and back to the scrubby helicopter landing field. At no point had I been told in advance where we were going or what we were doing. I did not mind. It was all fascinating to me, the glimpses of Mount Hermon, the unkempt but alert Israeli soldiers, the tidier Lebanese servicemen, the atmosphere of casual efficiency laced with perpetual tension.

We ascended into the air once again, our prayer-blessed helicopter taking us over terraced cultivation and over Arab villages which, even though composed of hideous cement houses, somehow sat fluently on the hillsides. There were neat orchards and, now appearing regularly, mosques, with domes coloured green or turquoise, to show that we were in an area inhabited by Shi'ite Moslems. This was rough country, with hills separated by deep ravines and decorated with handsome and effective drystone walling. The border commander pointed out to me, on a nearby hilltop, a huge building, a modern and well-equipped medical centre, built by a millionaire, one of the many rich men whose handiwork we were to see that day.

We landed on another hilltop. This was completely covered by the buildings and equipment of a huge, heavily fortified Israeli military camp. The Star of David flew defiantly over Lebanon. More to the purpose were heavy fortifications, a barbed-wire fence that looked as if it meant business, and special gates to guard against cars filled with explosives. We were met by Colonel Zviki, the brigade commander for the Awali River sector. The brigade in question was the Golani, one of the crack units of the Israel Defence Forces. Zviki, who might have been in his early thirties, was meticulously neat, ruddy-faced through perpetual exposure to sun and wind, and with the creases of constant smiles around his eyes.

He welcomed us and took us into a hut. Its walls were covered with maps. Its table was covered with food. It was a feast. There were apples drenched in chocolate. There was chocolate cake. There were sweets. I asked if these riches had been obtained locally from the Lebanese and was met with hurt stares. Nothing, but nothing, was bought from the Lebanese. All this had been made by the camp chef, a young man who was produced so that I could see that he really existed. It was at that point that I noticed the blintzes, sweet blintzes flavoured with chocolate, delicious blintzes, blintzes in Lebanon.

I was given a briefing in that heavy, dutiful way that is characteristic of Israelis determined to explain something. I was told that we were fifty miles inside the country.

'We cannot be the policeman of Lebanon,' said General Yomtov.

'There is no entity of Lebanon,' added Colonel Zviki.

'The Druze, the Shi'ites and the Sunnis are all out to kill each other,' chimed in Teddy, a perky young Intelligence officer, born in America and, as I was to learn, always more than ready to have his say.

So we set out by car, with a heavily armed escort, to see

for ourselves. The country was beautiful, staggeringly so. We went through a little town that started with a roadside Christian shrine, continued with a New Grand Hotel, and concluded with a Skylab Restaurant. Then we were up in the hills, with amazing panoramic views of the Awali River valley. The roads were lined with cypress trees; the variety, I was smugly told, was Jerusalem cypress.

'Very nice country, Lebanon,' said Zviki. 'Not place for war.'

And indeed we were tootling along as if for a placid country drive, occasionally meeting Lebanese civilian traffic which certainly benefited in one way from the absence of a properly constituted government. No-one, I was told, paid any kind of car tax. There was no official authority to whom to pay it.

We approached the large town of Jezzine, where, I was told, some 10,000 Maronite Christian Arabs lived. They seemed, however, to be idol-worshippers too. As we entered Jezzine, I saw women praying at a very large and ornate shrine dedicated to the Madonna of Jezzine. However, only a moment later there came into sight a building whose roof was dominated by the largest portrait of anyone that I had seen in my life. The subject was Bashir Gemayel, the murdered President of Lebanon, whose picture, indeed, had also adorned much of the available wall space during our drive and was even pinned to tree-trunks.

This was the mountain resort which in the later stages of the Israeli withdrawal from Lebanon, somewhat after I was there, was flooded with 50,000 refugees from Christian villages. Jezzine when I saw it was quiet, placid, even complacent. We sped through the town, giving me only a moment in which to notice quite well-stocked boutiques along the Rue General de Gaulle. Then we were out again, passing under a huge cross on a hilltop, overtaking a Druze riding a donkey, and finding ourselves among bleak, rocky mountains. It was all rather depressing, and Zviki did nothing to cheer me up by mentioning, as an incidental aside, that an ambush could happen at any minute.

It was, accordingly, a relief suddenly to arrive at an Israeli command post where soldiers in mountain combat dress clearly meant business and seemed well able to look after themselves and, at least as important, us. We had come to a point only six kilometres away from the limits of Israeli-held territory, a mountain pass where merchandise was transferred from one zone of Lebanon to another. All this was organized by two men called Levine, Lebanese Jews from Beirut whose considerable wealth had been destroyed by the PLO and who had escaped into Israel as soon as the arrival of Israeli soldiers made that possible. Now, combining the utterly irrepressible trading instincts of Lebanese and Jews, they were doing their best to make another fortune here.

They courteously paused to chat to me and, indeed, to attempt to tell me their life stories. However, out of the corner of their eyes they were watching various employees supervising, with the aid of soldiers, the transfer of goods from one set of lorries to another. No lorry was permitted to cross into one zone and out of the other, for fear of sabotage. So the lorries parked in ranks, back to back, and the merchandise was shifted from one set of vehicles to another, item by item, and checked to make sure that all items made the crossing. There were all kinds of things taking this hazardous journey. 'Those look like ironing boards!' I exclaimed incredulously. 'They *are* ironing boards,' confirmed one of the Messrs Levine, to whom ironing boards were a serious matter.

We left these assiduous people at their tasks, and continued on our way. Suddenly, we swerved off the road, drove up a bank, went through a gate, and found ourselves in wonderland. Here, in the middle of the mountains, was a palace; or, at any rate, an unfinished palace. It was ornately decorated, with filigree stonework whose fashioning must have turned many artisans blind. The walls were built in green, white and orange stripes. There were roaring lions and rampant winged gryphons. There were windows decorated with the most delicate trees. There were pillars and pediments and mosaics. There were cool archways and Oriental ovoids. Through unglazed windows the mountains seemed to be surrounded by picture-frames. One of the rooms included a

Star of David, and I asked what on earth this was all about. This, I was told, was a palace that a local millionaire, a doctor from Jezzine, had been constructing for twenty years and which might not be finished for another twenty, if ever. There was to be a room dedicated to each of the major religions, but at present there were no ceilings to separate these faiths from the sky. I got out my camera to photograph everybody in this suitable ceremonial setting, and we went on our way.

We arrived, before long, at another mountain pass. After watching the zealous activities of the Levine brothers, I had asked to be shown a place where people, as distinct from articles of commerce, crossed from one zone to another. My hosts, whose enthusiasm and good nature turned this whole hazardous outing into a kind of breezy day trip, had instantly changed the itinerary to fulfil my wish; and here we were.

We were higher than we had been before, nearly three thousand feet above sea level, and the soldiers here were dressed very warmly. We were lucky it was so mild today, I was told. Often there was snow. Here arrived buses going from the interior of one zone and into another. Civilians wishing to make the crossing got off the buses and walked in single file along a narrow walkway with metal rails on each side. They then entered a hut, where they were searched, and passed through to another vacant space, a few hundred yards farther on, where other buses were waiting to take them onwards. A file of people, men, women, lively children, was waiting to make the crossing. They seemed to accept this limitation of their movements in their own country as perfectly natural, waiting docilely to be searched and apparently quite content with the procedure.

A glum-looking soldier, ostentatiously armed, was perched in a hut on stilts up on the hillside. It looked like something Tarzan might have built for Jane. I made ready to take a picture of him. Ofra immediately told me not to, saying that he was a military secret. It was her only act of restriction the whole day and, since she told me very little about what was going on – not surprisingly, since she had only just taken up her appointment – I was not sure what useful function she was there for; she was, on the other hand, very pleasant, so her presence was a gain even if she had little in particular to do.

Deprived of picture-taking, I turned to a little Israeli soldier and decided to have a chat with him. I chose fortunately, since he spoke English well; indeed, he told me without delay that he had an uncle in Manchester. His name was Shmuel Paz, and I asked him what he felt about the war. He smiled; indeed, he looked as though he had never stopped smiling at any point in his life.

'The war itself was just,' he said. 'We had to come in.' This was an answer clearly satisfactory to those in authority; except that little Shmuel then added: 'But we didn't have to stay.'

I said goodbye to him, and promised to give his best wishes to his uncle from Manchester if I could find him (Shmuel was not exactly sure of his address). We proceeded on our way. Cherry trees lined the road. General Yomtov puffed at his pipe. We went slowly along a precarious road right at the edge of the mountain crest and my Israeli companions spoke in critical terms of the road-making talents of the Lebanese.

We paused to view another sight, of which the Israelis were as proud as if they themselves were responsible for it. Here, next to each other at the end of a sheer drop, were four gorgeous villas, built of local stone, erected by four wealthy Druze brothers. They dripped with rose gardens, and the only real question was how regular household supplies were provided for these mountain eyries. On the other hand, television reception must have been superb, even though, from what I had seen, the most easily accessible television programmes seemed to be tapes from America of large women wrestling with each other.

Our little convoy – we in our car, a radio car, and a protective jeep – suddenly came to a stop. We had met a large, bearded man coming the other way, an Israeli soldier who stopped for a word with Zviki. It turned out that he had come to the end of his tour of duty. I asked him what his conclusions were.

'I agree with the objectives,' he said.

'What are the objectives?'

'To keep Israel safe.'

It came as little surprise to learn that he was sorry to be going home. It was less of a surprise to discover one reason he was sorry to be leaving: the army food was better than at home. It was even less of a surprise to find out that he came from a kibbutz (run by Orthodox Jews), since many kibbutzniks have learned how to grow food but fewer have acquired the knack of cooking it.

We drove on for a while, and then once again swerved off the road. Zviki led us through a scrub patch, littered with bits of food wrapping and cigarette packets, and then stopped. We were at the edge of a sheer drop and below us, stretching for miles, was a view of the Awali River valley that looked as though it had been painted as a relief map. On this clear winter day, with the sun bright but not oppressive, the sight was idyllic. All was soft and green, with a huge forest in the foreground. The mountains benignly rimmed the valley and at the bottom, in a natural basin, the Awali River itself snaked along, a little like the Colorado in the Grand Canyon, glinting where the sun caught it.

So we returned to the Golani Brigade's encampment, to the hut where earlier in the day we had had our coffee and blintzes. Not a square inch of the table was visible under a banquet which would have seemed bounteous in a Tel Aviv luxury hotel. We ate, in a businesslike manner, speedily and fairly silently. Then I started on them. I wanted to know what they thought about being where they were, marooned on a mountaintop far from home, in a land where they had no business to be, cold, lonely, and with nothing much to do when it got dark except watch television and hope that they would not be bombed. Round the table sat Brigadier-General Yomtov, Colonel Zviki, Captain Teddy, the Intelligence Officer, Yitzhak, Yomtov's aide, Zvi, the helicopter pilot, and Ofra.

Teddy talked most. Indeed, I could hardly silence him and at one point had to tell him to shut up. He was nice enough not to mind and self-confident enough not to pay much attention anyhow. Yomtov said flatly that Israel had to go into Lebanon. The PLO forces had to be cleared out, and if the invasion had not taken place in June 1982 it would simply have had to happen later.

'What about withdrawing?' I asked him.

'That depends on the politicians. I'm a soldier and I would be ready for a phased withdrawal now. But we were right to go as far as we did. The Lebanese were simply unable to deliver what we needed.'

Next to him Zvi looked sceptical. It was because I wanted to hear what he had to say that I told Teddy to shut up. All the rest of them round the table were regular soldiers. The pilot was a reservist, a student at Jerusalem University.

Said Zvi: 'Whatever my opinion when it started, I now think the entry into Lebanon was a just act. But I want a phased withdrawal. And it should start right away.'

Zviki, who was nice about everything, was nice about this as well. He was also firm. He had no doubts at all: 'It was right to go in. It was right to go as far as we did. We should not withdraw without an agreement with Syria.' He was not to know that before long his government would decide to withdraw without any agreement with Syria.

Yomtov, as befitting the man with the most senior rank, was more judicious under questioning.

I challenged him: 'Here you are, an officer in the Israeli Defence Forces, yet in charge of an invading force. How can you justify that?'

'It was a question of the safety of the people behind the border,' he replied. 'We had to make them safe from the rockets of the PLO.'

'Yes, but you know as well as I that the border had been quite quiet and that you have lost far more killed in this war than were killed by rockets in the settlements. In Israel's other wars the existence of the state was in danger. Can you honestly say that about this war?'

Yomtov was frank: whether judiciously frank or recklessly frank I was not sure. 'No, the integrity of the state was not involved, only the security of the Northern border. The question was how to deal with this issue.'

The lot of them, then, were sure that Israel had been right to go into Lebanon, but not all of them were sure that it was right to go as far as they had. Most of them, only Zviki disagreeing at all, believed in a phased withdrawal at some stage.

One person, however, had remained silent. I turned to Ofra: 'You haven't said anything. What do you think?'

Ofra looked down at the tangerine peel on her plate. 'I will not give an opinion,' she said. 'I am simply a sad woman.'

That was really that. We all rose. Zviki and I went off to be photographed together standing next to the banner of the Golani Brigade, a huge green tree in foliage. Then, waving goodbye, we got into our helicopter and were whirled away.

We flew only a few feet above the peaks of the rugged, barren mountains of the Jebel Baruk. The Syrian forces were within shooting distance. Damascus was only 15 miles away. The mountains fell away, and we were over ploughed fields, the ploughing a little crazy, looking like whorls on the bark of a tree. Suddenly the ploughing changed. Now it was almost obsessively tidy, as if programmed by computer. We were back over Israel. We flew over Kibbutz Gonen. Said Yomtov: 'We take all visitors here to show what it is like to live under the nose of the Syrians.'

We landed at Mechanayim. I said goodbye to Yomtov, thanked him for the trouble he had taken with me, wished him good luck. It was still and quiet. I sat in a hut waiting for the Cessna to be readied for flight. This time I was going to Jerusalem. This time we were flying south, along the route of the River Jordan. At this northern extremity the river looked like a narrow canal, its banks lined with fields intensively cultivated by neighbouring kibbutzim and *moshavim*. Once again we came to the Sea of Galilee, the Kinneret. In the late winter afternoon it sat there threateningly, its surface a chill glaciation. White clouds sat in the sky and were reflected with precise exactitude in the water below. I felt as if we were flying between two heavens, one above, the other beneath.

Now the Jordan could be seen again, curving and turning,

not as straight a line as is shown on some maps. We passed over the town of Tirat Zvi, carefully planned, a hexagon inside a hexagon, from the air neat and symmetrical, on the ground no doubt as chaotic as anywhere else in Israel. We went over Beit Shean and its superb Roman theatre. On our left now was the Kingdom of Jordan, remote and unattainable, but seeming almost near enough to touch. Its hills were black but sun-kissed, looking like Plasticine models. The Jordanian fields were well-cultivated, apparently with some covert co-operation from the Israelis. There was a ribbon of towns along the foothills which ran down to the river. On the Israeli side the Jordan was bordered by a bright yellow line, the strip of sand placed there as a security barrier and no doubt lethally mined.

Then we were over the barren desert of Judea, where people could get lost in a few hours and die of thirst or exposure quite soon after that. There were signs of desperate attempts at cultivation by the Israelis, but the yellow desert won almost every time. The clouds were thicker now, but broad golden shafts of light forced their way through, making the scene look like a nineteenth-century Biblical etching. To the left a grey blot appeared, the Dead Sea, and above it the green splash of Jericho. A Roman ruin appeared, the remains of a fort. The canyons of the desert suddenly gave way to tower blocks, faced in golden stone and resembling a series of fortresses, rank upon rank. This was East Jerusalem, taken over by the Israelis who lived in these barracks and multiplied. We landed at Jerusalem Airport. It was 4.27 p.m.

I had been on my travels for eight hours and 42 minutes. I had been in a wild, lawless and dangerous land where I could easily have been killed, as others had been before I went and many others were to be afterwards. I had flown above most of the inhabited surface of the land of Israel, in all its moving beauty, and seen clearly what those soldiers risking their lives in Lebanon believed they were fighting to protect.

They were nice people, and most of them were very young. It was not only Ofra, however, who was sad. All of them

were sad, whether they knew it or not, whether they acknowledged it or not. For more than twenty years I had met
and spoken to Israeli soldiers. I had seen them in the West
Bank, in Gaza, in Sinai. All of them were sure they were
right to be there, none of them had any doubts of the justice
of their fight and their presence. For the first time ever,
Israeli soldiers were not sure about what they were doing
or why they were doing it, not sure that their war was just,
not sure that there ought to be a war. They fought bravely
and loyally when called upon to fight. They deserved better
from the politicians who had plunged them into ambiguities
so different from the certainties to which young Israelis had
been accustomed. Their doubts, their misgivings, the questions they were finding it necessary to ask and having to
answer, were a reflection of the uncertainty and self-question-
ing of the troubled nation of which they were the flower
and, God help them, the hope.

11

Down to Earth

It was time to leave. The women at the duty-free booths in the departure lounge were as off-hand as women at all duty-free booths in all the departure lounges in the world. In my aisle seat in the Boeing – a 707 this time – and as far as possible away from the statutory howling baby, I began to try to sort out what I had seen and heard, what I had been told and what I quite deliberately had not been told, during these exhausting but indispensable weeks.

That sourness which I had detected on recent visits to Israel was still most decidedly present. Yet I now realized that what was going on in the country was far more complex than I had anticipated. The state of the nation was perhaps even more worrying than I had thought. Yet, while there was cause for deep concern, for depression, even for anger, there was something else present too.

There was no doubt in my mind that Israel was being let down, badly let down, by its governments. The Labour Party, to which my sympathies automatically attached themselves, was at once too timid and too calculating. Having, to its surprise and shock, been turned out of what it had regarded as its rightful position as the perpetual government of the country, Labour had still not come to terms with the reasons for that displacement. Too many of its leaders believed that a little juggling with electoral arithmetic, a little pandering to this pressure group or that, could rebuild the political force that had dominated the country since long before Independence had been achieved in 1948.

Labour's bureaucrats did not understand that, in a political sea filled with scurrying minnows, their party had surrendered its dominance as master of the ocean and become simply one of two fairly big fish. Elections in Israel were no longer built round the question of how many of the smaller parties Labour needed to win over in order to form a majority; instead, it was in bitter competition, on almost equal terms, with another party capable in favourable circumstances of forming a coalition too.

Labour had still not reconciled itself to the fundamental changes in ethnic structure which its own generous immigration and absorption policies had helped bring about. It still could not accept the brute fact that the Sephardis were no longer a collection of squabbling minorities who could be played off against each other, but a preponderant sector of the electorate with urgent demands and a history of disappointment in obtaining satisfaction of those demands from the party which, in any other country, would have been their natural representatives. Israel's mass socialist party, dominated by intellectuals, kibbutzniks, part of the urban middle class and organized trade unionism, was unacceptable as the representative of the urban poor.

The Likud, for their part, were a collection of opportunists, without any discernible principles or programme and with few leaders of any particular ability, who had yet been shrewd enough to see the gap in the political market caused by the failure of the Labour Party to respond to the needs and aspirations of the Sephardis. A party originally composed of extremists that might well have continued in the future as what it had been in the past – a natural minority grouping with no hopes of sharing in government except in times of grave national emergency – had been transformed into a party of government regarded as equal to the establishment foe it had never imagined it could defeat.

The politicians had failed their electorate. Yet that was far from being the only failure. For the electorate – the people – had failed their country too. They demanded too much. Israel had no natural resources, no reliable sources of wealth, no industrial or agricultural products that could not be obtained elsewhere by importing countries in other parts of the world. There was some technological ingenuity, and revenue to be obtained from selling the advanced armaments which Israel had had to invent and manufacture for itself because of the unreliability of outside suppliers. Israel, in fact, possessed a hand-to-mouth economy unable by itself to sustain a high standard of living for its people. Such standards as existed – and they were pretty high – came courtesy of the generosity of outsiders.

Yet the electorate insisted on the maintenance of those standards regardless of whether they could be afforded. They demanded the television sets, the cars, the home computers that were manufactured by the developed nations of Western Europe, North America, and the Far East. They refused to accept the economic sacrifices which were necessary if Israel was ever to attain a realistic economy. When in mid-1985 the government introduced an economic austerity package with the modest goal – though monumental task – of reducing the annual inflation rate to around 100 per cent, the instant response of the Histadrut trade union movement was to call a twenty-four-hour general strike. The voters played off the competing parties to obtain what they coveted, believing that they were getting the better of a Peres or Shamir, when they were really only damaging themselves.

In a period when their internal economic problems and their external security problems demanded strong government, they luxuriated in preventing strong government by voting self-indulgently for small parties representing bizarre interest groups. By doing so they made their problems even worse, for the proliferation of small parties prevented their governments, whichever of the two main parties was dominant at any given time, from having clear and discernible policies. So when the world's only Jewish nation was in constant danger of destruction, its Parliament was forced to debate recondite questions of who was or was not a Jew. When the future of the West Bank of the Jordan was crucial to the security of the state, fringe religious groups compelled the extension of settlements on the West Bank by money-grabbing fanatics. A country whose founders had balked at mentioning God in their Declaration of Independence was now at the mercy of exponents of the doctrine of a vengeful, even a genocidal, deity. Most Members of Parliament, regardless of party, considered such developments as dangerous absurdities. Nevertheless, most Members of Parliament debated them as if they were central matters rather than marginal, if often perilous, distractions.

There was a nexus of deception between politicians and electorate, each tricking the other into more risky ventures. The voters demanded absolute security of a kind that was impossible in a country surrounded by enemies. The governing politicians responded by enormities such as the invasion of Lebanon. The electorate, provided with more than it bargained for, was then compelled to accept the justifications of the politicians for what they had done and, justifying itself for the dismaying response to its demands, to punish those opposition politicians who criticized what any rational person knew should never have been done. Begin and Sharon were primarily responsible for the carnage of the Lebanon war. Yet the voters were even more to blame, for Begin and Sharon were simply responding to what they thought the voters wanted, and the voters could have stopped it if they had really wished.

The Israelis were schizophrenic. They could not agree on answers to simple questions. Are we rich or poor? Do we want peace or war? Are we one nation of many kinds of Jews? Or are we many nations of Jews living together in one land?

And what was this land? There it sat, as I had seen it recede from the window of the Boeing 707, a thin, exiguous strip on the eastern shore of the Mediterranean, farther east than Egypt, than Cyprus, than most of inhabited Turkey. It was rent by political and social divisions caused by the emergence as a majority within the population of Jews of Sephardic origin. Yet those Sephardis were really its natural inhabitants, at home with its indigenous food, its geography, its terrain, its climate. It was those who had founded it as a modern state, the Ashkenazis, who were really the Israelis who did not fit in, who in their concert halls and museums and art galleries tried to pretend that they were really still back in Vienna or Berlin, that this untidy fragment of Asia was actually part of Western Europe. They were so persuasive that the Sephardis, too, wanted their state to be a Western state, even though they themselves were not truly comfortable in such a place. To call them Orientals was regarded almost as an insult rather than recognition of their peculiar suitability to live in and indeed to rule their country.

Israelis, leaders and led, were involved in a massive act of self-deception, of unrealistic role-playing in a country where brutal real life was outside every door every day. There was one aspect, however, of these people's relationship with their country that was very real indeed. All of them – Ashkenazis and Sephardis, Labour and Likud – loved their country. They loved it with a dedication and profundity unknown even among the most patriotic in any other nation in the world. When a war came, these people had to face the possibility of dying for Israel. Many people in many lands may say, and may mean, that they are ready to die for their country, and are never called upon to act in accordance with their words. For forty years, with heart-breakingly brief intervals between them, Israel's wars have required its tiny population to die for their country, and that population has accepted that requirement, readily. When Israelis say they are ready to die for their country, they mean it – and they show that they mean it by doing it.

That love of country has been, and will continue to be, the salvation of Israel. The problem of this land is not simply that it has never known peace. An even greater problem is that, with a small minority of exceptions, it is a nation of immigrants, of people who came from a hundred other places to make a new nation. Its Jews have successfully but artificially adopted a national language, Hebrew, but brought with them to this country dozens of separate, imported languages which many still speak among themselves and read in non-Hebrew newspapers. Moses led his people through the wilderness for forty years, so that the generations which had known exile and alien ways could die off before the Jews reached the Promised Land. The bewilderment and confusion which beset modern Israel are caused by the necessity for its perplexed and anxious Jewish inhabitants to live out their wilderness years right there, *inside* the Promised Land.